HELOISE AND ABELARD

by

Étienne Gilson

ANN ARBOR PAPERBACKS
THE UNIVERSITY OF MICHIGAN PRESS

Fourth printing 1972
First edition as an Ann Arbor Paperback 1960
All rights reserved
ISBN 0–472–06038–4 (paperback)
ISBN 0–472–09038–0 (clothbound)
Published in the United States of America by
The University of Michigan Press and simultaneously
in Don Mills, Canada, by Longman Canada Limited
Manufactured in the United States of America

CONTENTS

CONTENTS

Introduction

WHEN I announced in the Calendar of the Collège de France for the year 1936–37 a course of lectures on *The Medieval Origins of Humanism*, it was not difficult to foresee that I should have to deal with Abélard. This indeed is what happened. On the other hand, I was very far from realizing that I should have to devote quite as much attention to Héloïse as to Abélard himself, and that, once entered into their story, I should find it very difficult to leave off, not only because it is, indeed, so fascinating in itself, but because it is a kind of touchstone serving to test and evaluate the various definitions of the Middle Ages and the Renaissance which turn up from time to time. I have, accordingly, gathered together in the following chapters the essential material of the lectures given in 1937 at the Collège de France on this celebrated story. I am very far from considering them the last word on the question. Quite the contrary; I publish them in the hope of making it clear that the real problem has perhaps never been understood. Certainly it has never been interpreted from what was undoubtedly the point of view of the actual protagonists in the drama. I am referring, of course, to their ideas as they themselves understood them.

From the moment we approach it under this aspect, it becomes evident that, far from being able to arrive easily at its complete solution, we lack almost everything which might permit us to discuss it objectively. First of all, we are without a good text. There is no critical edition of the correspondence of Héloïse and Abélard. We shall see, in the last chapter of this work, how serious can be the consequences of a mere change of two syllables in the text at present at our disposal. We urgently await the services of the critical edition of the correspondence of Abélard and Héloïse undertaken by the Pontifical Institute of Mediaeval Studies of Toronto. Unfortunately, there is only a small number of French manuscripts available to establish this text: those of Paris, Bibliothèque Nationale, 1873, 2544, 2545, 2923 (once owned by Petrarch), 13057, the fragmentary 13826 and the two folios of 20001; a Troyes manuscript, 802, basis of our printed text; a Rheims manuscript, 872, and Douai 797. Perhaps there are in France other manuscripts not yet identified; and there is good reason for thinking that there are some to be found elsewhere. Rawlinson's edition,[1] published in 1718, claims to be based on a manuscript placed at his disposition by a friend. Several readings of this English manuscript are exceedingly curious and do not turn up again in any French manuscript we know. But where is it? Some claim that it has never existed. This may be the case. But it is just possible that we have not here to deal with a myth and that some day someone will find it. On the other hand, we know that the Troyes manuscript, 802, which came from the Library of the Chapter of Notre-Dame de Paris, was purchased in 1346, along with four other volumes from the same source, by Roberto de Bardi.[2] Roberto, who became Chancellor of the University of Paris in 1336, was an Italian, a friend of Petrarch,[3] and the same who, in 1340, invited the poet to come to Paris to receive the crown of laurel which he, however, preferred to receive at Rome.[4] Thus, of the three best manuscripts of the Correspondence known at present, two belonged to the Italians of the fifteenth century: to Petrarch and to one of his friends. Moreover, we know that Coluccio Salutati asked Jean de Montreuil for a manuscript or a new copy of the correspondence in 1395 and that the work was sent to him, perhaps in Florence, in 1396.[5] If, as is undoubtedly the case, this manuscript reached Italy, where is it? These are some of the questions—and others could be asked—which will one day perhaps receive their answer. Those who, perchance, find themselves in possession of the answer can be assured that their information will be gratefully received at the Pontifical Institute of Mediaeval Studies, Queen's Park Crescent, Toronto, Canada.

A critical edition of the text of the Correspondence is not the only tool we lack. We should still have to be able to read it. Now the *Historia calamitatum* raises historical problems so numerous and of so varied a nature that no one can boast of possessing all the techniques necessary to solve them. History of facts, history of ecclesiastical institutions, canon law, history of classical literature and of medieval literature, history of philosophy, history of patristic and medieval theology, indeed, everything has a place in it. The worst of it is, everything dovetails. A mistake in Latin or ignorance of a fact can at any moment entangle the historian who is guilty of them in a series of arbitrary interpretations

whose brilliance will never compensate for their futility. I
do not claim to have avoided all these pitfalls, but at least,
I have desired to carry the examination of problems, as far
as possible, into fields where I have no special competence
so that, even if I am misled, their urgency and scope will
henceforth be unmistakable.

These, however, were accessory problems which only
arose for me in a functionary capacity with another all-
important one: the philosophical and theological ideas running through these facts, determining them or at times motivating them, giving them life and ever tying them together, giving them, in fine, the meaning which these dramatic events had in the eyes of those who found themselves
involved in them. Such is the proper object of the studies
which constitute this volume. I should be only too willing to
announce that my present subject is the ideological back-
ground of the story of Héloïse and Abélard. But the doc-
trinal convictions of the two lovers, along with the purely
human passions which are here released, form its real basis.
This, at least, is what I believe, and it is at the same time the
only thing I really hope to have demonstrated.

Thus understood, this essay on a famous correspondence
really belongs with other essays on the dealings which philosophy has with literature in any age. I wanted to leave
with it the character of the lectures which it substantially
reproduces. The courses offered by the Collège de France
are public, but without any sacrifice of technical character.
There is no affirmation unaccompanied by justifying references and, if possible, by proofs. I am not unaware of the
disfavor with which certain literary opinion eyes books
burdened with notes. A contemporary essayist, giving

promise of a brilliant career,[6] speaking in my presence, said
of the author of two huge erudite volumes: "What a pity
he has piled up so many references! When you have finished reading the book, you would like to rewrite it and
make something worth while of it." A recipe more often
followed than one thinks; as if it were enough to relieve a
book of its notes to endow it with style! Here, then, is a
little book full of notes. They are no pledge of its style, but
they are of its honesty.

Besides, if it is merely a question of literature, Abélard
has been profusely covered with it. This in no way suggests
that all that has been written is bad. There are some things,
indeed, quite excellent, and curiously enough, it is from
England that we have the best. The insipid and frequently
ridiculous *Imitations*, in verse, by Beauchamp, Colardeau,
Dorat, and Mercier, in the eighteenth century, are in no
sense comparable with Pope's epistle, "Eloisa to Abélard."
I would not take an oath that Pope is always faithful to the
thought of Héloïse. But I know at least four of his lines
which Héloïse herself would have been sorry not to have
written, so well do they express what the Abbess of the
Paraclete suggests on each page, without daring to give it
expression:

> Still on that breast enamour'd let me lie,
> Still drink delicious poison from thy eye,
> Pant on thy lip, and to thy heart be press'd;
> Give all thou canst—and let me dream the rest.

If this is not what Héloïse was thinking as she wrote Letters
II and IV of the Correspondence, then it is useless for other
poets to try to express her experience. The last line, espe-

cially, is priceless. In prose, one ought also to read the
Héloïse and Abélard of George Moore, whose fluid and
musical prose style moves with measured rhythm, a trifle
slow, perhaps, but wisely regulated from the first to the last
page of his two volumes. But above all we should not forget that vital, charming book, penetrating and infinitely
more faithful to reality than George Moore's, the *Peter
Abelard* of Helen Waddell, author of *Wandering Scholars*
so familiar to medievalists. Indeed, English literature has
paid greater tribute to the memory of Héloïse and Abélard
than has our own.

I rather feel, however, that France has done better in the
field of pure history, and that this somewhat dramatic adventure has been better told there and the psychological
analysis of the characters more intensively developed.[7] The
most complete work yet written on Abélard is probably
Charles de Rémusat's *Abélard, sa vie, sa philosophie et sa
théologie*, the second edition of which is dated 1855. On
the two volumes of the copy which I have before me appears the signature, "Aloys de Pourtalès, Neuchâtel, 1866".
To bear the name of Héloïse and to dream of the old in a
place so rich in memories of the new, how eminently fitting! But no Héloïse appears on the cover of de Rémusat's
book. There is only a hooded Abélard, sinister monk, reading the Bible among the graves. It is indeed Abélard who
is the hero of this book. In spite of some academic ornamen-
tation, the history of his life as told by Charles de Rémusat
seems to me to surpass, in shrewdness of analysis and wealth
of historical information, all other accounts of a similar nature which I have been able to consult. Others will perhaps
be able to do better, but nothing will ever dispense the

scholar from consulting it, were it only to read pages like the following about the feelings of Abélard.

"Some critics have reproached him with being unable to endure the absence of her whom he had too much loved. And I doubt whether they were telling the truth. It appears, on the contrary, that his soul, hardened and chilled, was sensible only to sorrow. If we look more closely into the source of his thoughts, we can, in the reserve of his language, in the cold and cramped kindliness of his bearing and expressions, everywhere detect a certain deliberateness, and so guess what a struggle was produced in his soul by smarting regrets, by bitter shame, by respect for himself, for religion and for the past, perhaps, too, by the vague fear of the weakness of his own heart. All these pent-up feelings he carries over into the attentive and delicate solicitude of the director of conscience. To outward appearances he outlines for his religious and for their abbess only evangelical exhortations, monastic rules, letters of spirituality, all that piety and learning dictate. But there reigns in all this so tender though restrained a sympathy, so evident and so lively a preoccupation with all the interests confided to his care, and at the same time, wherever it was a question of general truths and the philosophy of religious life, a confidence so absolute, and so intimate a need of being heard and understood, that we cannot assist at their strange and final transformation of love without a blending of consternation, pity and respect." Here is an illustrious example of what neither de Rémusat nor anyone else has ever been able to prove and which nevertheless thrusts itself with the force of genuine evidence on every sensitive ear as soon as the texts of Abélard have become familiar to it.

After reading de Rémusat's book on Abélard, it is well to read also Miss Charlotte Charrier's on Héloïse.[8] Not only will we find gathered here a considerable body of documents on the misfortunes of the two heroes in the course of their posthumous fame, but we will have the pleasure of seeing a woman resolutely taking the part of the woman against the man and avenging, in the name of her sex, the unfortunate victim of Abélard. Nothing could be more moving or more sincere than this indictment, full of feminine charges against a wretch guilty of unpardonable crimes and unspeakable meanness, but who, be it said, has too dearly paid the price. It is hardly necessary to go on berating him, even in our day. It is true that Héloïse suffered a great deal, and suffered because of Abélard, but two things at least are certain: that she would have done ten times over what she did, were she free to climb ten times the same Calvary; and that she would have resented as the worst of injuries our daring to exalt her by disparaging Abélard. I don't think she would have permitted another woman to lift a hand against her idol. It is impossible to give adequate expression to what would have been the response of Héloïse's hand to Miss Charrier's book.

When all is said and done, the Correspondence is the only work which it is really necessary to read in order to understand this drama.[9] It is a human document of such wealth and beauty that it may be duly ranked among the most moving pieces in all literature. I remember now the day when, in the manuscript room of the Bibliothèque Nationale, I shamelessly molested a kindly scholar, a perfect stranger to me otherwise, but whose Benedictine habit marked him as my victim. I wanted him to decide on the spot and without delay the precise sense of the words *conversatio* and *conversio* in the Benedictine Rule. "And why," he asked me, "do you attach such importance to these words?" "Because," I replied, "on the sense of these words depends the authenticity of the correspondence between Héloïse and Abélard." Never did a face express greater surprise. Then, after a silence: "It is impossible for that to be unauthentic. It is too beautiful."

Neither one of us took this judgment for a proof, but we knew very well that it was true. For this Benedictine scholar was not speaking so much of beauty of style as of beauty of souls large enough to have been promoted to such sufferings. Here the scholar in him knew a great deal less about it than the Benedictine.

I

The Sources of the Drama

SAVE for Abélard and Héloïse, we are practically without witnesses to teach us the history of their drama, and
so far as concerns its sources, we have only the testimony of
Abélard at our disposal. Let us add, however, that the pitiless penetration of his self-analysis is of such a character as
to inspire us with confidence and that no known fact from
any other source entitles us to contradict anything he says.

At the moment when the drama, whose ideology we are
undertaking to analyze, takes place, Abélard had already a
long and tumultuous history behind him. His trials, however, had as yet only been those of an ambitious young
genius, busy carving out for himself the place to which he
had a right, and thrusting himself naturally against the obstacles which his elders put in his way. Henceforth, he
could enjoy his triumph in peace. All his rivals had been
vanquished, eliminated, and for several years now he had
been the undisputed possessor of the title of Master in the
Schools of Paris which destiny had long since assigned
him. There he was teaching theology and philosophy with
equal success. The unusually large number of students who
crowded eagerly about his chair was accompanied by a cor-

respondingly large amount of money and by general ac-
claim. All this he tells us himself. But Foulques of Deuil
confirms it with great profusion of details and in the most
formal manner. There is no reason to suppose that Abélard
is not telling the truth on this point or that much has been
exaggerated.[1]

The immediate effect of Abélard's extraordinary success
was to aggravate that pride from which he had never been
entirely free. Here again, he is himself the accuser, and we
can take his word for it. "I was of the opinion that there
was no longer in the world any other philosopher but myself."[2] This he confessed much later on. But long before
Abélard admitted it publicly, Foulques had already bitterly
reproached him for it.[3] The same weakness naively makes
its appearance in the *Dialogue* where he has the Greek philosopher with whom he is conversing extol his fame.[4] Along
with pride and money there comes, inevitably, luxury. So,
after four or five years of unprecedented scholarly triumph
(1113/4–1118), temptation came his way, and before very
long, he yielded to it.

If we had to believe Foulques of Deuil in the matter, Abélard would seem to have had many other affairs besides that
which was so tragically to link his lot with that of Héloïse.
Charles de Rémusat, prudent and delicate as he is in his
analyses, appears to have been convinced by Foulques' testimony.[5] Miss Charrier, only too pleased with this opportunity of attacking Abélard to let it pass, does not hesitate
to quote Foulques as saying to him: "What caused your ruin
was the love of women and those licentious ties in which
they had entangled you."[6] As a matter of fact, Foulques'
testimony is somewhat different: "What, as they say *(ut*

aiunt), caused your ruin is the love of all women *(singularium feminarum)* and the snares of desire with which they catch libertines." Here we see, in the first place, that it is a question of a "they say". Foulques is not speaking as a witness. Secondly, his sentence expresses less a precise fact than a general idea. Dissolute as one might suppose him, no one will believe that Abélard loved "all women" *(singulas feminas)*. Let us grant that Foulques wished to accuse Abélard of running after women and, as he adds later on, of thus ruining himself.[7] But the fact remains that in this text it is only a question of rumors which pursue him. *As they say, as I have been told, as it is said* are but so many reservations by Foulques himself on the value of his evidence. Surely the only fair procedure is to record them as such.

Let us go further. Objections against Foulques' charges are not wanting. First of all, Abélard has accused himself of worse failings, but never of this one. He tells us, and it is a point whose significance in his eyes we shall see better later on, that before seducing Héloïse, he had led a perfectly chaste life. "I, who had led up to then a life of continence, yielded my loins to lust."[8] What is more, Abélard precisely states that he had always had a horror of prostitutes and that he would never have fallen from the sublime apex of continence—weighty expression of an import we shall have to recognize—had not ill fortune offered him in Héloïse the occasion to fall from it.[9] For him as for her, it was a first fall: "The less experience we had of these pleasures, the more ardently we sought them."[10] Abélard's ardor was that of a beginner. Did his horror of courtesans disappear after the seduction of Héloïse? It is only too possible, but he has

nothing to say about it himself. Heloïse could not have
been ignorant of so notorious a misbehavior as Foulques
imputes to him, yet she never uttered the slightest reproach.
Finally, even Roscelin, in his ferocious and occasionally
filthy letter where he speaks as an eye witness, makes not
the slightest allusion to these supposed disorders. Moreover,
as Roscelin tells him, it is quite unnecessary to resort to in-
vention in order to expose his baseness; it is enough to repeat what everyone from Dan to Bersabee already knows.
Roscelin relates this, certainly not without speaking of a
courtesan, but only of one, *scorto tuo*,[11] Héloïse. One who
did not hesitate to hurl this insult at Héloïse was hardly the
man to spare Abélard. Foulques' hearsays have little weight
before the silence of an adversary like Roscelin.

From Abélard's own point of view, the seduction of
Héloïse, as he himself relates it, was a sufficiently vile affair
without gratuitously charging him with any others. There
was not the least trace of romantic passion so far as he was
concerned, nothing but lust, as he admits, and pride. "Flat-
tering fortune provided a more favorable opportunity"
(Fortuna blandiens commodiorem nacta est occasionem).
Héloïse was above all only too convenient an occasion to
let pass. She was "not ugly of countenance" *(facie non
infima)*—hence his lust. When Abélard met her, she already
far surpassed in knowledge all other women of her time—
and thus his pride. We must not forget, indeed, that Héloïse was already famous throughout France even before
knowing Abélard personally. She herself recognized this
and Peter the Venerable, much later, reminded the Abbess
of Paraclete of the fame that had been hers from her youth.
It has been charged that Peter only wished to console her

by flattery. This is possible, but flattery is not always untrue. Since he here speaks as a personal witness of Héloïse's renown, to contest the value of what he says[12] we have actually to accuse him of lying, not merely of flattery.

Whatever may be the case, Abélard himself suggests clearly that the learning and reputation of Héloïse were not the least of her attractions. "She had a rather lovely face, and was unrivaled in the breadth of her literary culture." Let us add to this that everything concurred to make of her a victim especially prepared for the eyes of Abélard. He had a horror of prostitutes, yet his life as a professor kept him at a distance from the daughters of the nobility and bourgeoisie. Héloïse was like neither. She moved in a circle all her own. In the first place, she was lettered. Abélard could write to her—a factor which always simplifies such affairs. Then, she was niece of Fulbert, cleric and canon like Abélard himself, and moved in that special little world of which the cloister of Notre-Dame was the center. Once Abélard had chosen his victim, or better, when circumstances had presented her to him, nothing was easier than to arrange a meeting. He had his friends present him to Fulbert, took lodging with him, and used the avarice and vanity of the uncle to have him entrust his niece to him for her education. Already so celebrated for her learning, what might she not become under such a master! From that moment, Abélard had won a partial victory. Sufficiently handsome, as he modestly states, that he need not fear the refusal of any woman, this brilliant master was assigned from that moment, by an uncle blinded by pride, the right to direct day and night the studies of Héloïse, and even to administer corporal punishment if he judged it advisable. Executioner and victim conspired to judge it advisable, if only the more easily to deceive Fulbert. This whole coldly calculated plan is unfolded before us in the *Historia calamitatum*. It is no love story, but the tale of the incontinence of Abélard, victim of the noonday devil. But here let us pause and set it down to his credit that it is Abélard himself who furnishes us with all this damning information. He has his vanities and his failings, but he is no prevaricator. It is most unlikely that he is trying to deceive us. If it were merely a question of telling this story so as to exculpate himself from all blame, who could do it better than Abélard might have done?

Considered from the viewpoint of Héloïse, the problem is only too simple. There is nothing to be said save that she allowed herself to be seduced. No word of Abélard's warrants our supposing that she offered the slightest resistance. Everything she says later suggests that she was overwhelmed by the aureole of fame hovering over the Master. "Whatever you wished", writes the Abbess of Paraclete later on, "I blindly carried out." It is the same theme, and we have no reason to think that this was not the case from the beginning. Somewhat later, however, we do find Héloïse suffering scruples and putting up some resistance. But this is looking too far ahead, and the passion which was to dominate the whole life of Héloïse seems, indeed, to have been complete from its very beginning. This passion must not have been long in conquering the seducer himself. For after the seduction of Héloïse, Abélard was no longer the cold calculating person that he had been at first. The two became happy lovers. As much more eager for these pleasures as the pleasures were new for them, they served the apprenticeship of carnal passion without any other master than nature, and perhaps Ovid. This first happiness was to be also the last.

These new pleasures, which neither of them ever denied afterwards, were not, however, without their counterparts. In the first place, Abélard, victorious, soon experienced the usual effects of such victories. His case is a classical illustration of what the authors of courtly romances call *le cheva-lier recréant*. Unsatisfied passion is a source of exaltation and heroism, but the lover's victory frequently deflates him. Abélard began now to forget his obligations, to neglect his courses, and to forsake his schools. In the place of commentaries on Aristotle and the Scriptures, he composed love songs in honor of Héloïse. In short, from philosopher and theologian he became a poet, and he had enough judgment left not to regard the change as an improvement. Above all, what had to happen did happen. Uncle Fulbert was demonstrating as much blindness as he had shown imprudence. As Abélard says, citing St. Jerome, we are invariably the last to know what is going on in our own home, and everyone knows what a woman is up to before her father or her husband notices anything amiss.[13] If we remember, however, that all this was taking place under Fulbert's roof, we shall not be too surprised to learn that after several months of these carryings on, the same thing happened to them, Abélard relates, as happened to Mars and Venus when they were surprised by Vulcan. A glance into Ovid will explain this figure.[14] This accident, only too inevitable, inaugurates the era of their tribulations.

After such a scandal, they had to separate. But far from putting an end to their passion, this separation only aggravated it. From this moment the two lovers rebelled against morality and against public opinion. It is true that immediately after their discovery Abélard was very much ashamed, but as soon as secret encounters again became possible, passion removed all vestiges of shame and the irremediable character of the scandal created rendered both of them insensible to it. Nothing better demonstrates their complete indifference not only to religion but to morality and even to public opinion than Héloïse's sentiments on realizing that she was to become a mother. She wrote about it to Abélard in cheerful raptures. Whereupon, profiting from an absence of Fulbert, Abélard had her abducted and sent her into Brittany to the home of one of his sisters. Free rein is given to the imagination of novelists who describe this voyage. Indeed, all we know about it is that Abélard had her travel disguised as a religious. This detail will have some significance for us later on. It was in the home of Abélard's sister that Héloïse brought into the world a son to whom she gave the pedantic if perhaps symbolic name of Astrolabe.[15]

It is not surprising to hear that after this abduction Fulbert fell into an indescribable rage bordering upon madness.[16] But what could he do? Nothing, certainly, so long as Héloïse was in the hands of the relatives of her ravisher. After some delay, Abélard felt at last that he could seek out Fulbert, acknowledge his crime, make his excuses and ask his pardon, pleading for his defense that love had always been the ruination of great men and offering to repair the wrong he had done. What he offered was to marry Héloïse under the one condition that their marriage be kept secret. We are today so far from these events and we live in a world so different from Abélard's that the meaning and value of such an offer, made under a restrictive condition of this nature, escapes us almost completely.

To discover a meaning in Abélard's proposal, we have available two equally astonishing clues. First, Abélard affirms that going of his own accord to offer to marry Héloïse was to offer Fulbert a satisfaction beyond anything he could have hoped for; secondly, that in compensation for this unlooked-for offer, Abélard was asking that his marriage be kept secret, "so that my reputation should not suffer thereby".[17] Such expressions suggest that the marriage was possible, but that it was of a character altogether abnormal, of a nature to cast a reflection, if divulged, on the good name and reputation of Abélard. It seems immediately evident that Abélard closely associated these two factors, not only with each other but with his position as regent of the schools of Paris. Now our only precise information on this subject is that afforded by one of Héloïse's objections to this projected marriage: "you, cleric and canon".[18] Our only hope, therefore, of clearing up so obscure a question rests on these two words.

First, what was a cleric in the period when Abélard bore this title? He indicates himself in one of his sermons that the cleric is one who is tonsured and whose rank is the lowest in the ecclesiastical hierarchy; that is, below porter.[19] Abélard noticeably hesitates to decide whether the state of cleric is the lowest of ecclesiastical orders or something inferior even to the lowest.[20] In any case, it is certain that for him a simple cleric is one who has received tonsure, who has not yet received any ecclesiastical order, not even the lowest of minor orders, that of porter. No document, no text at present known, authorizes us to suppose that at this time Abélard had received any order, even minor, nor that he was, whatever it means, more than a simple cleric, that is, tonsured.

It does not follow from this, however, even from the point of view of the Church, that his state of life was devoid of all rank nor free from all obligation. According to Isidore of Seville and Ivo of Chartres, tonsure, by which one becomes a cleric, is a symbol of continence.[21] He who receives it is one of those whom God has chosen as His part and who have themselves chosen God as the part of their inheritance. "Clerics . . . that is, chosen ones", says Peter Lombard later on, following the tradition of Isidore and St. Jerome.[22] Such being Abélard's state of life, in what way could a public marriage have prejudiced his reputation?

One might first reply that in the twelfth century every professor of philosophy, and, *a fortiori*, of theology, was a cleric; and that by marrying, Abélard would lose his clerical status and consequently also his right to teach. With marriage, therefore, his career would come to an end.[23] But even here there are several difficulties. The first is to ascertain whether the marriage of a simple cleric dissolved his clerical status. As a matter of fact it does not appear that this was the case. Ivo of Chartres lists several cases in which a cleric lost his status and became once more a simple layman; some of these pertain to marriage, but none corresponds with Abélard's case. For example, a cleric who married a widow, that is, a woman living in the continence of her widowhood, lost his clerical status. So, too, did an adulterous cleric.[24] But a cleric, after consulting his bishop,[25] could validly contract marriage, and the fact that he was thus married was so far from dissolving *ipso facto* his clerical status that if he showed signs of abandoning his tonsure and becoming once more a layman, his tonsure was reimposed. This is what Ivo of Chartres expressly recalls on the subject of simple clerics—*sine gradu*—who have been authorized to marry and who have given up their tonsure. "Let him be forced to receive tonsure again, and let him not dare to neglect his tonsure as long as he lives," states Ivo's text. "If he abandons his tonsure, let him be tonsured again."[26]

It is clear, therefore, that Abélard's difficulty, if he married, would not have been to retain his clerical status, but to lose it. However, if the preceding texts do not support so simple a solution of the problem as might be hoped, they do suggest another, much more complex, but which might very well be the right one. Although it may have been legitimate, the married cleric's status appears to have been a kind of makeshift. After all, even married, the tonsured person still wears, or at least ought to wear his tonsure, symbol of continence. He is therefore in a rather perplexing position, as is clear from the canonical texts where the problem is dealt with. Can a layman who has remarried receive tonsure? The *Decretum* of Ivo of Chartres says No. This is an overstatement. Let such a one remain a layman: "A concession granted generally because of human frailty is one thing, a life consecrated to the service of the things of God is another."[27]

In other words, for a married layman to become a cleric or for a cleric to marry are tolerable contingencies; but a widowed layman who remarries shows himself from the moment of this second marriage incapable of remaining continent and at the same time unsuited for clerical life,

which is by definition a life consecrated to the service of
God. All this seems to imply that for the cleric anxious to
respect the dignity of his state the position of the celibate
cleric far surpasses that of the married one. This is a point
to which we shall have to return, but it is perhaps useful to
quote here a text of Abélard himself defining as clearly as
possible his own point of view on this problem of canon
law. According to him, one who has secretly taken a vow
of chastity and feels incapable of observing it, can impose
a penance on himself and marry. Those who have taken the
same vow publicly, as, for example, monks or priests, cannot contract marriage. Orders, then, are an impediment to
marriage; however, those who have received minor orders
up as far as acolyte can be validly married if they renounce
their benefices. On the other hand, those who have received
an order above acolyte cannot marry.[28] This stated, it still
remains true that the marriage, although valid and licit, is
a makeshift. It is the remedy for a weakness, a concession
made to the incontinent as a bulwark against their incon-
tinency. To this should be added that the remedy imposes
a mutual servitude on the two spouses, and that every wise
man, solicitous for his liberty, ought to avoid it. A wise
man should not marry.[29]

Abélard's position, then, is quite clear. Everything he
says about it indicates that from his own viewpoint the marriage of a cleric was a valid and licit act but that the marriage state very much resembled a fall from grace. Since
the canonical texts agree with what Abélard says, there is
no reason to suppose that he wanted to keep the marriage
secret because it would have been illicit, but everything
points toward that "loss of glory" which he dreaded in

the moral lapse which the marriage of a cleric suggests.

The second question to arise is whether Abélard in marrying was losing his right to teach. We can readily understand how this might be the opinion of those who think that marriage dissolved the clerical state;[30] but if it is established that marriage did not dissolve it, there seems to be no reason why this cleric should have been deprived of his offices. It is true, as we have just seen, that a simple cleric who married lost his benefices. But we are not aware that Abélard had any benefices to lose. The money he earned came rather from his numerous students than from any other source. It was only later on, when he had become a monk, that he refused to accept money from his auditors at the Paraclete. Again, and this is more important, if it had been a question of this, Abélard would not have demanded a secret marriage "to avoid loss of fame", but "to avoid loss of money". It is necessary then to search in another direction.

We should be on much more solid ground, and different ground too, if we could prove that a cleric who married, even though he did not lose his clerical status, did nevertheless lose his right to teach. Of course, a married professor of philosophy and theology would have been an extraordinary and undoubtedly unique phenomenon in the Middle Ages. But then, everything is extraordinary in this story. The chief question is to know whether this extraordinary phenomenon was possible. Nothing justifies our saying that it was not possible, and many things entitle us to believe that it was. We can easily see how ecclesiastical authorities would have been anxious to remove from the immediate service of the altar married clerics not in major or minor orders. However, in 1031 the Council of Bourges conceded

to priests, deacons and subdeacons, married and deprived of
rank because they refused to leave their wives (or con-
cubines) the right to continue performing the functions of
lector and cantor.[31] Similarly, the *Decretum* of Ivo of Chartres, which forbids the marriage of deacons, does not forbid
that of lectors; and the *Decretum* of Gratian charges even
lectors to carry out their obligation to choose between the
vow of continence and marriage.[32] In brief, as Génestal
observes: "The marriage of the cleric beneath the rank of
subdeacon is not only valid but licit; the cleric who con-
tracts it must not be guilty of any lapse; and Gratian has
collected texts to this effect—not only can he, but he must
continue the functions of the clerical life."[33] If it was indeed thus, it is impossible to see how the marriage of Abélard, even if made public, could have kept him from teaching. The tendency, more and more marked from the time
of the early Church, of removing married clerics from the
immediate service of the altar, can have no force here, because a lector or an acolyte still performs liturgical functions corresponding to specific grades in the minor orders;
but a simple cleric has received no order, even minor—
clericatus non est ordo—and a professor does not exercise
even the modest functions of porter. He does not teach in
the church. From whatever point we consider the problem,
there seems to be no reason why the public marriage should
have deprived him of the right to teach.[34]

An examination of this problem from the point of view
of the persons most concerned brings us to the same conclusion. As we shall presently see, Héloïse never for an
instant believed that the secrecy demanded by Abélard and
promised by Fulbert would be kept. She had excellent rea-

sons for not believing so, and that is why she always looked
to the future realistically; not from the point of view from
which Abélard would have things, but from the point of
view of things such as she knew they would be. Thus it is
interesting to observe that desirous as she was to avoid this
marriage, Héloïse never had recourse to this very simple
argument: if you marry me your career is finished, for you
will no longer be able to teach. If the argument had been
possible, it would have been decisive. The fact that Héloïse
does not use it encourages us to believe that it was impossible. Indeed, in a celebrated passage to which we shall have
to return, Héloïse undertakes to describe how strange will
be Abélard's life the day when, married and living with his
wife and children, he must teach philosophy *and theology*.[35] Undoubtedly Héloïse only depicts this life in order
to make it distasteful beforehand, but the fact that she undertakes to emphasize its drawbacks, or even its impro-
priety, suffices to prove that she considered it *possible*.
Neither Héloïse who paints this picture, nor Abélard who
reproduces it for us, imagined for an instant that the publicizing of their marriage would put an end to his teaching
or that his students might then desert his courses. Héloïse's
chief concern is, not to know whether there will be any
students, but to know where to put them. What is more,
she was right. Married, handicapped, ridiculed, persecuted,
Abélard will not be so sheltered in the solitude of the Paraclete that students will not flock to him. The marriage
may be a reflection on his reputation, but not on his reputation as a professor.

There still remains the title of canon. We know a great
deal less about this than we do about that of cleric. But we

do know, at least, that we have to lay aside the notion of canon which arises naturally today; that is, of the incumbent of a rather dignified office and, *a fortiori*, a priest. Abélard himself speaks to us of numerous canons who were in rebellion against the efforts of their bishops to make them accept sacred orders.[36] The proposal only began to interest them when it was a question of their becoming bishops. We must also distrust the notion, a great deal more tempting, that Abélard was necessarily a member of the Chapter of Notre-Dame. Those who speculate whether he was a canon of Tours or of Sens rather than of Paris, seem to have something like this in mind.[37] At the period in his career which we are here considering, he was certainly a canon of Paris. But what does this title mean?

The strongest reason, or the most tempting, inviting us to make Abélard a member of the Chapter of Notre-Dame, is that every chapter included a *scholasticus* among its dignitaries; and we know, moreover, that Abélard was then directing the schools of Paris: "While you were presiding in the schools of Paris."[38] It would seem, then, to be natural to identify the regent of the schools of Notre-Dame with the *scholasticus* of its chapter. There are, however, certain difficulties with this. There is scarcely any doubt that the duties of the *scholasticus* of a chapter originally included the direction of the schools of the episcopal cloister; but it would be imprudent to conclude from this that the *scholasticus* of the chapter had the right to be regent of the cathedral schools. The texts which Du Cange cites in his article on *scholasticus* are all later than the twelfth century; moreover, it is very dangerous to conclude from the practice of Cahors what was taking place in Paris. In one of these texts, dated 1252, we find, not a *scholasticus* but a "master of the schools", whose principal function was to name a suitable person "to rule the schools in his place." In another text of 1288, there is indeed a *scholasticus;* that is, there is a man "by whom even the rector of schools is to be appointed." In a third text, undated, borrowed from the "Ancient Statutes" of the church of Frankfort, the *scholasticus* teaches grammar and supervises the good order of the choir. He sees that all kneel together, stand up together, sit down together; in effect, he is a master of ceremonies. There is nothing here to suggest a necessary or strict relationship between this title and the duties of the regent of the schools.[39] Since we know so little about this office in Paris during the first third of the twelfth century, it is impossible either to affirm or deny that Abélard was *scholasticus* in the Chapter of Notre-Dame, or that he was *praelatus,* or that this dignity involved the duties of the master of the schools or was independent of them. His title of canon can be explained with much less trouble.

From the beginnings of the Middle Ages the bishops had been preoccupied with introducing more order into the life of the secular clergy.[40] The expression in use to designate the kind of life they wished to impose on the secular clergy was *vita canonica;* that is, a life conforming to the canons of the Church. Hence, for example, the *De institutione canonicorum* of Aix-la-Chapelle (817) was clearly intended to remind clerics, and indeed all Christians, of the essential precepts of the Christian way of life. The clerics to whom these regulations were addressed were not monks, but they were organized into communities governed by very strict rules and bore the title *canonici.* They were called canons, their life completely regulated, but they remained secular clerics. Beginning from this epoch, the Church clung to this ideal of a secular clergy canonically organized. Limiting ourselves to dates relatively close to the epoch which concerns us, let us recall that the Lateran Council (1059) prescribed anew for all clerics in major orders the regular, common life.[41] Such was the ideal, though actual practice was far from conforming to it. The ideal itself varied considerably according to time and place, and the Church's very insistence upon renewing her prescriptions attests the resistance she was encountering.[42] In practice, the cathedral chapter included an indefinite number of clerics of every rank bearing the title of canons, not because they were a part of the chapter or bound by the canonical rules governing the life of the clerics, but because they performed one function or another in the cathedral church or its dependencies. The cathedral schools were directly dependent upon the bishop; and the regent of these schools must have borne the title of canon, probably with a benefice.[43] The simplest hypothesis is that Abélard was one of these. The title certainly carried a number of obligations and conferred on him a certain dignity; but canons of Paris were not rare. Foulques of Deuil speaks of them as multitudinous: "The multitude of noble canons", he writes, "are raising a complaint."[44] A married canon regular would have been a real scandal; a married canon who was but a tonsured cleric, like Abélard, would have been in an unfortunate situation, particularly if he were a celebrated professor. His ecclesiastical position would certainly have been affected. He would even have found himself ecclesiastically

thing like this. They have not said that by marrying, Abélard was going to lose his last chance of one day being Pope, Cardinal, or Archbishop of Paris. And even had they admitted that by his marriage he would lose the benefice attached to his canonry, as well as the canonry itself, we should still not know that he expected to obtain either the one or the other. But we are perfectly sure that as a cleric, legitimately married, Abélard might, if he wished, have continued to perform his functions of cleric in teaching philosophy, or even theology, which he certainly wanted.

Rather than attribute to them motives which neither have admitted, we ought perhaps to pay attention to those which they have confessed. De Rémusat knows these very well. He actually summarizes them. But he sees in the arguments by which Héloïse tries to dissuade Abélard from the marriage only a "strange discourse"; and he even describes her passionate plea as "that odd sort of argument."[2] Héloïse's objection to Abélard's proposal was that a philosopher born to serve mankind, a cleric who has given himself to the Church, had no right to bind himself with the bonds of marriage. Odd or not, it is Héloïse's actual argument. And Abélard's shame is that, wanting the courage to avoid the marriage, he tried rather to keep it a secret. The two lovers were in agreement about the ideal for both the philosopher and the cleric, and it is to Héloïse's credit that, after their fall, she did all in her power to encourage Abélard to return to his ideal. To neglect as simply a curious accessory this ideal itself, to refuse to see in it the hidden force which exalts and governs this whole conflict, while Héloïse and Abélard speak of nothing else and judge the affair only in relation to it, is to miss the very gateway to the moral

labyrinth within which it is still so difficult to find one's
bearings. Wherever their reflections take them, Héloïse
and Abélard are preceded, followed, even pursued by the
overwhelming shadow of St. Jerome, which Abélard had
no doubt himself conjured up before the mind of Héloïse
and which her very uprightness no longer allowed her to
forget. "St. Jerome, the greatest Doctor of the Church and
the glory of the monastic profession",[3] such is the great
man among the great, the master among masters whose stature is the measure of all height and all depth. It is not a
question of knowing whether, in marrying Héloïse, Abélard was sacrificing a prebend or a mitre, but whether or
not he was demeaning himself. The real force of Héloïse's
arguments is that so long as Abélard was free he could still
become, if not a St. Jerome, at least a Seneca; but in marrying he was cutting himself off from the heroes of the spiritual life and all hope of return would, from that moment, be
denied him. The whole force of Héloïse's arguments, and
well she knows it, depends on the fact that they challenge
Abélard by confronting him with an ideal which she had
learned from him and which, as we shall see later, he never
abandoned.[4]

St. Jerome's testimony on Seneca, whose influence on
Abélard's attitude was decisive, is worth reproducing here
in full: "Lucius Annaeus Seneca, of Cordova, disciple of
the Stoic Solion, paternal uncle of the poet Lucan, led a
life of very great continence (*continentissimae vitae fuit*).
I should not inscribe his name in the catalogue of sacred
authors, if the letters, so widely read, from Paul to Seneca
and Seneca to Paul did not invite me to do so. Although he
was Nero's instructor and a very powerful person in his

day, Seneca states there that he would like to hold among
the pagans the same place Paul held among the Christians.
Two years before Peter and Paul received the martyr's
crown, he was put to death by Nero."[5]

It follows from this text, first, that St. Jerome had sufficient confidence in the apocryphal correspondence between Seneca and St. Paul to give this pagan philosopher a
place among the authors whose work is significant for the
history of the Church.[6] It follows secondly that this pagan
"St. Paul" could be considered, even by the Christians, as
a model of continence. Had St. Jerome some precise information about the life of Seneca? It is doubtful. His remarks on Seneca's life are probably based on his philosophy
and on the kindly hypothesis that Seneca's life was in line
with his teaching. It is not, in fact, impossible to piece together a eulogy of chastity from Seneca's writings. He
ranks chastity among those goods the loss of which renders
death preferable to life, and chastity *(pudicitia)* occupies
in his doctrine an equal place with liberty and wisdom.[7] No
slight praise this! Nor was Seneca the only pagan whom
Jerome could cite in support of chastity. The long fragment of Theophrastus' treatise *De nuptiis* has been translated by St. Jerome and is not otherwise preserved.[8] But
the text as we have it is quite adequate, and shows that Abélard and Héloïse had meditated on it at leisure. The question asked by Theophrastus was: Should the wise man
marry? And the reply: No! Because it is so rare that all
the conditions requisite for a good marriage are present in
the same case, and even when they are, it is still better to
refrain. Why? Because a wife prevents a man from attend-
ing to philosophy, and because it is impossible to serve two

masters, one's wife and one's books. Wives are always wanting something. Deprived of it, they pass whole nights in
endless complaining. Why did you stare at that pretty
neighbor? What were you saying to the little servant girl?
To feed a poor wife is a burden, but what agony to support
a rich one! If she is beautiful, men run after her; if she is
ugly, she runs after men. One has either the task of keeping what everyone wants or the annoyance of keeping what
no one wants. In short, Theophrastus advises the philosopher not to take a wife but to get a good servant.[9] Whereupon St. Jerome cries: "When Theophrastus speaks these
things, and others like them, what Christians will not blush
for shame, above all those whose life is in heaven and who
say each day, 'I long to be dissolved and to be with Christ'
(Phil. 1:23)?" Héloïse has carefully collected both the
counsels of Theophrastus and the conclusion St. Jerome
draws from them, and directs their combined force against
Abélard's project.[10]

This is not all. Jerome had called on Cicero to support
Seneca and Theophrastus. After Cicero had repudiated
Terentia, his friend Hirtius offered to give him his sister in
marriage, but Cicero declined the offer under the pretext
that he was unable to give himself to both wife and philosophy at the same time. For the rest, St. Jerome adds
amiably, the admirable Terentia ought to have married Sal-
lust, sworn enemy of Cicero, then Messala Corvin, and thus
descend by stages the degrees of eloquence. Héloïse was
very careful to note this example of Cicero in order to send
it, as she had the others, to Abélard.[11] Let us add to these,
still of course with Héloïse whose arguments we but present, the story of Socrates who, when Xanthippe sprinkled

him with a foul liquid, had to console himself by saying that after such a storm one could expect it to rain.[12] There is a final and colorful picture of the practical incompatibility between philosophy and the domestic life. Héloïse herself supplies the details of the account, but St. Jerome has several times referred to it in his treatises and letters of direction.[13] If we but consult it, we will readily agree that it was Héloïse's opinion that Jerome strongly upheld the ideal of the continent philosopher which visibly haunted her. But we know that Abélard shared with her this same ideal. He could read the texts of Seneca where philosophical Stoicism became one with the prescriptions of Christian morality. For Abélard, Seneca always remained "that eminent votary of poverty and chastity, supreme moral teacher among all philosophers",[14] whose image St. Jerome had bequeathed to him. He was "that greatest of moral philosophers",[15] "outstanding for eloquence and moral teaching." He was the correspondent and admirer of St. Paul whose exemplary life Jerome had praised.[16] He was "Seneca, the greatest builder of morality", whose *De beneficiis* was to furnish similar examples for Abélard's sermons.[17] Again he was "that illustrious moralist," admirer and correspondent of St. Paul, and once more St. Jerome's account is reproduced in full.[18] He was "Seneca, among all philosophers, singularly gifted in the possession of moral doctrine delightfully combined with the good life", and he it was who in one of his letters to St. Paul clearly recognized that the Holy Ghost is the source of all goods.[19] In short, Abélard's picture of Seneca which came quite as much from his reading of St. Jerome as from Seneca himself, presents him as the moralist par excellence. Pagan antiquity placed before Abélard, under the approv-

ing regard of the greatest of the Church Fathers this model
of a doctor of natural law in whom philosophical grandeur
was inseparably wedded to moral continence.

Héloïse realized, therefore, that she was touching Abélard to the quick when she cited the following text from the
Letters to Lucilius against the proposed marriage: "It is not
only when you are a man of leisure that you must be a philosopher; you must neglect everything else to consecrate
yourself to it, for no amount of time is adequate for such a
study. . . . To interrupt philosophy amounts to not being a
philosopher, for from the very moment of the interruption,
philosophy vanishes. . . . It is necessary therefore to resist
other occupations. Rather than multiply them, fly them."
Thus, concludes Héloïse, what those who today truly deserve to be called monks undertake for the love of God, the
illustrious philosophers of the past undertook for the love
of philosophy.[20] Does not Abélard deserve to be placed
among these "famous philosophers"? For both Héloïse and
Abélard, this was the real question.

What Héloïse desired for the man she loved was, therefore, a state of life worthy of his stature as a philosopher.
Now it happens that the greatest of the apostles agrees on
this point with the greatest of moralists. Seneca teaches that
the true philosopher never ceases to be a philosopher; St.
Paul teaches that the true Christian never ceases to pray. So
here the Apostle of chastity adds the protection of his authority to that of the Moralist of continence. If you wish
to be a philosopher, says Seneca, hold yourself aloof from
all that is not philosophy—honors, public engagements, even
marriage. For marriage suffers when you love another
man's wife; and public honors and affairs suffer when you

love your own. If you must love, love reason;[21] therein lies
wisdom. Are you a Christian? adds St. Paul; hold yourself
aloof from all that might interrupt your prayer. Above all,
avoid marriage, not because it is to be condemned in itself,
but because it is an obstacle to the perfect continuity of the
Christian life. "He who is unmarried is concerned with
God's claim, asking how he is to please God; whereas the
married man is concerned with the world's claim, asking
how he is to please his wife; and thus he is at issue with
himself" (I Cor. 7:32–33). Now the teaching of St. Paul is
the basis of all St. Jerome's remarks on the incompatibility
of the married state with the perfect Christian life.[22] For, in
the last analysis, if what St. Paul has to say about the necessity of praying always is true, what are married people to
do? The very essence of the married state is against it. The
husband does not belong to himself, nor the wife to herself;
they belong to each other in the very strict sense that each
of the parties possesses rights to the very body of the other
which cannot be refused. He who marries gives up his
liberty: "Let every man give his wife what is her due, and
every woman do the same by her husband; he, not she,
claims the right over her body, as she, not he, claims the
right over his" (I Cor. 7:3–4). The married state, in its
very essence, involves this loss of personal liberty, and this,
let us not forget it any more than did Héloïse, was the firm
right, the definitive power which Abélard was going to give
her over his own person, and therefore over his life as a
philosopher, if he married her.

St. Jerome was here reminding Abélard that it was his
duty not to turn over these rights to Héloïse, and Héloïse
that it was her duty not to accept them from Abélard. "Do

not starve one another," St. Paul said, "unless perhaps you do so for a time, by mutual consent, to have more freedom for prayer" (I Cor. 7:5). The very liberty to pray is subject to another's pleasure. The one will not be able to pray, nor even remain with the disposition required for Holy Communion, unless the other is willing. What a strange bond is that for a Christian! "When I perform the duties of marriage, I no longer fulfill those of continence. In addition, the Apostle orders us, in effect, to *pray always* (I Thess. 5:17). If I must pray always, I must never marry, for each time I render my wife her debt, I can no longer pray."[23] Irrefutable reasoning, based on the mutual rights and debts which the sacrament itself confers on spouses, and which St. Jerome has summed up in a curt apothegm: "either we pray always and are virgins, or we serve in marriage and lose the liberty to pray" *(aut oramus semper et virgines sumus, aut orare desinimus ut conjugio serviamus).*[24]

If we accept all this as their honest view of what the philosopher and the cleric ought to be, everything they have to say in the matter becomes crystal clear. We, of course, live in times when this twofold ideal has lost its splendor; we refuse to take what they say seriously, and their story loses its true meaning. In order to supply it with another, the historian has to become involved in explanations which no text warrants. Héloïse never ceased to maintain that the marriage would be, for Abélard, dishonorable and a source of ever recurring difficulties: "she advanced at the same time my *dishonor* and the *difficulties* of the marriage".[25] The marriage, she said, would be infamous and onerous; in brief, it would bring disgrace *(turpitudo)* to Abélard—a disgrace which would affect her too since, in giving her irregular. But he would only have had to resign his office as canon in order to regularize his position.[45]

We do not deny that considerations of the above nature may have entered into Abélard's real reason for wishing to keep his marriage secret. But we shall have to look much deeper than to purely restrictive regulations, which may or may not have been felt to be really binding, if we wish to get at the heart of the matter. But if we insist on examining mere regulations, we must remember to put a minimum of emphasis on the letter of the law and a vast deal upon the religious ideals which dictated it.

II

The Secrecy of the Marriage

WHEN they reach the question of the secret marriage, the better historians give free rein to their imagination. If Abélard wished to hide his marriage, says Charles de Rémusat, it is because "this marriage was sacrificing something of his ambition; it was a course which could compromise his position in the school, force him at least to give up teaching theology, deprive him of his office of canon, close for him the path to high honors in the Church. Abélard was far from despising these things. Indeed he is said to have had ambitions to wear the mitre of the Bishop of Paris. Some have even spoken of the Roman purple. What say I? Perhaps the papal tiara itself".[1] Possible? Yes. Who could ever prove that Abélard did not cherish the hope of one day ascending the pontifical throne? And, since he would only be secretly married, might he not have quietly installed himself in Rome with Héloïse? One wonders if those who formulate these hypotheses make the slightest effort to grasp the sense of what they imagine. Perhaps it is sufficient criticism to say that these suppositions are irrefutable precisely because they are founded on nothing. Neither Abélard nor Héloïse ever hinted at any-

What gives it its force is that Abélard never for an instant dreamed of calling it into question. For him as for Héloïse, the clerical state is one thing, marriage another. He must choose between being master of himself or living in servitude, between practicing continence in order to have the right to attend to philosophy as a free man or of renouncing it and no longer teaching an ideal which he must admit being incapable of practicing. In speaking of marriage as "a yoke" *(de tanto matrimonii jugo)* and in speaking thus in the name of St. Paul, of St. Jerome, and of the philosophers whom St. Jerome had cited, Héloïse was challenging Abélard to practice what he taught. In urging him not to sanction his own lapse and not to impose upon her the shameful position of accomplice, she was appealing to something very powerful and very profound in each of them: the sense of his very real greatness, and the justification of his fame in the eyes not only of the Church but of the entire world.

Abélard never for an instant doubted that the marriage would be a humiliation and a servitude: "What bond is tighter than the conjugal yoke," he wrote later, "what servitude heavier for a man to bear than no longer to be master of even his own body? In short, what can be more trying in life than to be daily a prey to the cares of wife and children?" What is, after all, a husband? He is a "domesticated beast of burden".[34] Under the pen of Abélard, as of Héloïse and St. Jerome, the theme of the practical difficulties subsequent to the marriage of a cleric and that of its unseemliness or social inconvenience[35] are always tied up with the basic teaching of St. Paul on the corporal servitude of spouses and its essential incompatibility with Christian perfection. "Is there greater servitude for husband or wife than not to be master of their own body, than not to be able to abstain from carnal relations, even to pray, without the other's permission?"[36] Thus as St. Paul puts it, and Abélard never grows weary of quoting the text, since the body of the husband belongs to his wife as the body of the wife to her husband, the continence of each depends on the incontinence of the other. For marriage is a remedy against the eventual incontinence of either the man or the woman, and this is why each of the spouses must bow to the will of the other and must endure this "form of mutual servitude" (*mutuam quodammodo servitutem*)[37] which Héloïse may possibly have desired for herself but which she certainly did not wish for Abélard, and which she judged unworthy on Abélard's part to think of imposing upon himself.

If we admit that this was their state of mind, and we have their own word for it, the subsequent conduct of Abélard and Héloïse in this matter again becomes intelligible. To doubt that Héloïse could take these arguments seriously, or even, as has been done, that she could have actually borrowed them from St. Jerome, is simply to doubt that she was Héloïse. Her attitude and her methods are not assuredly those of the ordinary woman, but then, she was not an ordinary woman. That such a gifted and lettered woman used such arguments showed precisely that she was a woman. Moreover, from the time of her first reply to Abélard, Héloïse expressly acknowledged, and implicitly guaranteed as authentic, the array of arguments which the letter of Abélard publicly attributed to her: "You have rightly wished to recount some of the arguments by which I tried to deter you from our marriage and that fatal wedlock."[38] As though expecting that a precise argument against this double testimony might be produced by some historian, the whole text and its context invites us to accept it as faithful to the truth.

At the point we have now reached in the analysis of the texts, the situation can be thus summarized. Cleric and canon of Notre-Dame, Abélard could only contract marriage on condition that he resign his canonry. On the other hand, he keenly desired this marriage for more or less obvious reasons which he has saved us the trouble of having to guess. Abélard held an academic office, highly regarded at the time, chief of the schools of Paris, and he was intent upon retaining it. But he could no longer bear the separation from Héloïse; and to bring her from Brittany to Paris and to renew their liaison without stirring up to fever pitch the fury of Fulbert, he simply had to marry her.

We must here take into account, since Abélard has confided in us, the deep burning passion which had taken possession of him and bound him eternally to Héloïse from that moment. The cold calculation that had served his lust to effect the seduction had given place to an affection, violently carnal it is true, but whose carnal sincerity cannot be doubted since it was the cause of all his misfortunes. From that moment, Abélard loved Héloïse with a love exclusive and jealous, which rendered insupportable the thought that she might ever belong to another. He wanted her for himself alone, and forever. He wanted her in this way because he loved her; and the only means of holding her forever was to marry her: "because I loved you beyond measure and longed to hold you *forever*" (*cum cuperem te mihi supra modum dilectam in perpetuum retinere*). Sure of the present, he was jealous of the future—scarcely a noble sentiment, and even mean and base for one who knew Héloïse as Abélard must have known her, but one he experienced nevertheless, as so many other men would have done in his place, and which he never afterwards denied. Later, after the assault, when he was already Abbot of Saint-Gildas and she Abbess of the Paraclete, Abélard again congratulated himself, for Héloïse as well as on his own behalf, that their marriage had bound them one to the other forever. Even at this late date, after their tragic separation and entrance into religion, he had full confidence that Héloïse would still have married him, were she still free to do so. "If, indeed, you had not been married to me already, at the moment I left the world, you would have married me then, moved either by the suggestion of your family or by the seduction of your carnal desires."[39] Abélard was never more sincere than when he wrote these lines. Never does he more clearly show that he was unworthy of Héloïse, nor how much, on the plane of human love, he always lagged behind her. It is only on another plane, as we shall see later, that it will be given him to surpass her.

Meanwhile, it seems clear that Abélard's decision to marry was one which no one ever called sacrilegious, but which everyone judged extraordinary—Fulbert, because he found it so unexpected; Abélard, because it was far from his mind when he seduced Héloïse, and because even when he had decided upon it, he wanted it kept secret; finally, Héloïse, because she had allowed herself to be seduced without holding Abélard either to marriage or to the vaguest promise of marriage, and who even tried to dissuade him from it when he made the proposal. Now, up to the present, the texts at our disposal only authorize one single explanation of the abnormal and extraordinary character of this marriage, that offered by Abélard himself: "in marrying, I was destroying myself; I was casting a slur upon my own honor." On this explanation, we have only one authentic commentary, made by Abélard, each consideration of which he borrowed from Héloïse: that his true greatness as cleric and philosopher is inseparable from celibacy. This consideration Héloïse set forth in a later letter. She made Abélard aware of its real force and he attests himself in several texts that he acknowledged its validity. If history consists in retracing events as they can be known and interpreted from the only documents known to exist, then it is in the concept of the cleric which Abélard received from St. Jerome and in Abélard's ambition, if not to be a cleric according to the spirit of Seneca and St. Jerome, at least to pass for such, that we must look for the real reason for his asking that the marriage be kept secret. If it is merely a question of writing an historical novel, we can imagine a dozen more obvious reasons, depending upon the type of readers for whom it is written. As for internal criticism, which is so necessary and excellent so long as it uses one document in order to criticize another, eliminating from them what only appears to be true in order to discover what is really true, it loses all its value from the moment that it substitutes the point of view of the observer for that of the things observed. We have seen the birth of the "Critical Spirit" and all the pedantic fiction with which it encumbers history, fiction which at its best is not even entertaining. For it is characteristic of the "Critical Spirit" to be itself the measure of historical reality. When an event

surprises it, the event loses its right to have taken place.
When a sentiment goes beyond its grasp, he who expresses
that sentiment loses the right to have experienced it. It is to
be feared that this story of great souls, reduced to the stature of the scholars who write about it, is sometimes wanting
in graphic beauty, but it will inevitably be wanting in truth
when that truth consists in personal greatness. Héloïse and
Abélard are great, even in their faults; we cannot measure
the real depth of their fall save from the height of the ideal
to which they refer. This ideal is nothing less than the
heroic virtues of the Christian life. Both of them speak in
terms of these, not to sing their personal victory but to mark
the extent of their defeat. This is why they can be believed;
and no one who believes them can ever judge them as se-
verely as they judge themselves or refuse to grant them
what they hoped for in confiding in us, a little love and a
little pity.

III

Between Two Separations

In spite of Héloïse's obstinate objections, Abélard's will
finally prevailed. She loved him and he was the master.
If he wanted it this way, she had no other course. The
simple words with which Abélard records her feelings vi-
brate with truth and sincerity. "She could not bear to make
me suffer"—*nec me sustineret offendere.* Thus Héloïse
yielded, breaking into tears and saying with a sigh: "We
have no alternative but to become lost in each other and to
suffer even as we have loved." In this, adds Abélard, she
was once again moved by the spirit of prophecy as the
whole world has since recognized.

Their decision taken, the two lovers entrusted the child
to Abélard's sister and returned secretly to Paris. Several
days after their arrival, they passed a night of secret vigil
in a church and received the nuptial blessing at daybreak.
The only witnesses were Fulbert and a few friends of either
party. Soon afterwards, they departed separately. From
then on, Héloïse and Abélard saw each other but rarely and
secretly, taking every precaution not to reveal their marriage. At this time, Abélard must have been around forty
years of age, Héloïse about eighteen.

In deciding to keep their marriage secret, Abélard involved himself and Héloïse in inextricable difficulties. The marriage could not be an absolute secret, since Fulbert had to be present in order to assure himself that he was not being duped. He had even to demand the presence of other witnesses. It was most unlikely, human nature being what it is, that even one witness could have kept the secret. For several of them to have done so was entirely out of the question. Fulbert could be counted upon to see that the affair was noised abroad. Abélard must indeed have been swayed by violent passion to have been blind to such a risk. We can only conjecture at the cause of such lack of vision. The simplest hypothesis and, unfortunately, the most dishonorable, is that Abélard figured that his offer to marry Héloïse was sufficiently unexpected to purchase Fulbert's silence. Fulbert could hardly have hoped for such complete reparation. But from the moment that Abélard brought Héloïse back to Paris and refused to break with her, Fulbert was not only justified in hoping that Abélard would marry her, but it was his duty to demand it. If Abélard's calculation was based on what Fulbert might have expected, then he was really offering to exchange little or nothing for very much indeed.

But this is not all. In offering the secret marriage as reparation, Abélard was offering only private reparation for a public offense. Every cleric in Paris knew that Abélard had seduced Héloïse in the very house of her uncle, and that he had subsequently carried her off from under his nose. A secret marriage might satisfy Fulbert's moral sense, but hardly his honor. For the marriage to give anything like full satisfaction, it ought to be publicly known. The more

so in case the furtive and rare meetings of Abélard and
Héloïse became public knowledge. Otherwise Fulbert's
shame would be doubly grievous and Héloïse very seriously
dishonored. Abélard had not allowed her to remain his mistress, but he was, rather unscrupulously, allowing his wife
to run the risk of being mistaken for his concubine, and this
merely to save the façade of personal glory after the build-
ing behind it had collapsed. Abélard could count on total
sacrifice from Héloïse. She would never forgive us if we
doubted this. In the order of human love she was without
peer. But we could scarcely credit it, had we not his own
word for it, that Abélard could have counted on a similar
sacrifice from Fulbert.

But he did just this; and what had to happen, happened.
Uncle Fulbert and his associates, seeking to compensate
themselves for the affront received (writes Abélard indig-
nantly and with disarming naïveté) were not slow to break
their promise and to reveal the marriage. Héloïse, on the
contrary, played the game to the end. "She swore by all
her gods that nothing could be more false" *(illa autem e
contra anathematizare et jurare quia falsissimum esset)*. We
can easily understand Fulbert's anger at such obstinate per-
jury in publicly giving him the lie. He had not the same
reasons as Héloïse for loving Abélard. But it is only fair
to say that of all the forms of vengeance he might have con-
templated, the mere publicizing of the marriage was the
most innocuous. If they had only been wise enough to yield
on this point, Fulbert would probably have gone no farther.
But Abélard was adamant; and Héloïse did not yield an
inch. Violent scenes took place between her and her uncle,
scenes culminating in insults, possibly in blows: *crebris eam*

contumeliis afficiebat. Abélard was roused, and, to put an end to the situation, sent Héloïse to the Abbey of Argenteuil where she had gone to school as a girl.

Quod cum ego cognovissem, "having become aware of it", is what Abélard writes. There is no way of knowing whether there were other motives behind his decision, but the rest of the story is of such a nature that we can hardly help supposing others. Certainly he must have wished to remove Héloïse from the violence of Fulbert and to find her shelter elsewhere. Her former convent home, Argenteuil, was a very suitable spot, and it is more than likely that Abélard thought so. But there was danger here of making Héloïse's intentions appear ambiguous and of making Fulbert believe that Abélard wished to be rid of her by having her enter religion. Certainly, if Abélard wanted to make him think this, he would have acted in some such manner. It did not anger him to have this believed. Since both he and Héloïse still denied that they were married, he had not yet made the sacrifice of his personal honor as a cleric. But Héloïse had found it necessary to use some strong language about those who said she was married. This suggests that the rumor must have become fairly widespread. In sending Héloïse to Argenteuil, Abélard was taking two measures. He was protecting her from Fulbert; and he was putting an end to these rumors about their marriage. You can see that she is not my wife. She has entered the convent! I should not dare to attribute to him motives of which he has said nothing, did he not provide this somewhat disturbing detail: "I also had her take with her the religious habit, except for the veil, and I had her clothed in it."[1] I hesitate to translate the Latin text literally—*et his eam indui,* ("and I clothed her in it")—because it suggests that Abélard gave Héloïse the religious habit—without the veil—in a sort of formal ceremony. However, Héloïse could not pass in the eyes of the world as a novice. It is hard to believe that Abélard went to these lengths merely to simplify the question of Héloïse's garb behind the convent doors. Whatever his intentions, we can excuse Fulbert in permitting himself to be deceived about them.

The rest of the story is well known. Abélard tells us that when Héloïse's uncle and her relatives were informed of these facts, they thought Abélard had tricked them and that he had sought a means of easily ridding himself of Héloïse in thus having her enter religion. Violently indignant, they formed a counterplot against Abélard. Buying off his servant, they surprised him as he slept in a secret room in the quarters he occupied and cruelly and shamefully mutilated him. As he puts it himself unequivocally, and repeats it later on: they punished him where he had sinned.[2] Everyone, he adds, was stunned by this news. The following morning a mob formed, and joined its clamor to the even greater lamentations of the clerics, especially the students, and thus covered him with a shame far more unbearable than the physical pain he was suffering.[3] This time it was all up with his personal glory. It was gone forever. His enemies were triumphant, his relatives and friends dishonored, because the unusual character of the assault was going to call it to the attention of the whole world. How could he ever again appear in public? People would point their fingers at him, ridicule him as a curious kind of freak. All the texts of the Old Law where God Himself rejected eunuchs, excluding them from His service as unclean creatures, flooded his thoughts. The letter of the Law might now be abrogated, but it was always there as a living indication of his fall. Not knowing where to turn, and rather by shame than by religious vocation, as he tells us himself, he sought peace and silence in the cloister of the Abbey of Saint-Denys.[4]

It is well known that he was to find there neither the one nor the other. Urged to take up again his teaching of philosophy and theology, he composed at the abbey a treatise, *De Unitate et Trinitate divina*, which was condemned and burned at the Council of Soissons. To cap the climax, he succeeded in wearing out the patience of the monks of Saint-Denys, both by reproaching them for their morals—an easy matter for him now—and by proving to them that their abbey had not been founded by Dionysius the Areopagite as they claimed. So he fled from the abbey and, after many vicissitudes, obtained permission to retire near Troyes into solitude. He later wrote a eulogy in praise of solitude which Petrarch read and scored.[5] Before long, students came to people this desert where, lacking everything, too weak to work the soil and too proud to beg, Abélard agreed once more to teach in exchange for the food his students provided. Their cabins rose up near his own, and thus the modest oratory of earth and reeds which he had constructed for himself was rebuilt and enlarged. Originally he had dedicated it to the Holy Trinity, but he loved to speak of it, for the sake of the consolation he found there, as the Paraclete. His ever-vigilant enemies were scandalized, or pretended to be scandalized, by all this. Those who had remained his friends up to this time forsook him, and he lived now in such misery and fear that, whenever he saw an ecclesiastic arriving at the Paraclete, he was filled with terror lest he be dragged before a new council for condemnation. He was on the verge of despair at being suspected of heresy, and was considering flight to some pagan land where perchance he might be favorably received as a possible convert. But at this juncture he was unexpectedly informed that the monks of the Abbey of Saint-Gildas de Rhuys had chosen him for their abbot. This distant abbey in Brittany, hidden away in a country whose very language, he tells us, he could not understand, appeared little better than exile among barbarians. But it was an opportunity for further flight. So he abandoned the Paraclete to take refuge in a monastery where the monks were not only thieves but even, as he was to learn by bitter experience, assassins.

There was no common life at Saint-Gildas. Each monk was busy with his own purse and with the family for which he provided. When these new conflicts which Abélard had to carry on with his monks were at their height, he learned that the religious of Argenteuil, where Héloïse had become prioress, had just been expelled from their monastery. The thoughts of the Paraclete, standing desolate and deserted, had troubled him ever since he had left it. As the land belonged to him, and also the oratory and the few cabins which his students had erected, he decided to install Héloïse there with those of her sisters who wished to accompany her. Accordingly he left Saint-Gildas, went to the Paraclete and, with his Bishop's permission, gave it to the new community. The foundation was solemnly confirmed by a Bull of Innocent II dated at Auxerre, November 28, 1131. Although this Bull only gives Héloïse the title of Prioress of the Oratory of the Holy Trinity, she was to be and to remain for the rest of her life, the first abbess of the Paraclete.

We know nothing about their meeting after this long and painful separation. All that Abélard has to say about Héloïse at this time is that she was remarkably successful; that, after a difficult start in extreme poverty, help came from every direction; so much so, he says, that Héloïse accomplished more for her sisters in a single year at the Paraclete than he could have done for them in a hundred.

Their plight was much more touching as they were but weak women. But above all, everyone loved Héloïse, "who excelled all the rest" *(quae caeteris praeerat);* bishops treated her as their daughter, abbots as their sister, the laity as a mother. All admired her piety, her prudence, and the incomparable meekness with which she was able to endure all things. Continually occupied in meditation and prayer in the privacy of her cell, she rarely saw anyone; and the very rarity of her interviews only made outsiders seek her the more eagerly.

After giving the sisters this property, Abélard apparently held himself aloof for some time. Whatever his policy, of course, he was bound to be in the wrong. First, he was reproached for neglecting the new foundation, for failing to assist it at least by preaching. Whereupon, he began to make frequent visits and to preach not only to the sisters, but to outsiders as well in order to encourage others to help them too. We still possess a sermon of his delivered on one of these occasions.[6] We can only surmise what embarrassment it cost him to undertake this kind of preaching. Then, as we might well expect, pious souls began to be scandalized. Some charged that now, more than ever, he needed Héloïse. Abélard at first was consoled by the knowledge that St. Jerome had not escaped such calumnies. But he confessed some surprise that he was not, under present circumstances, spared such reproaches.[7] Following this remark, we find him dwelling upon texts concerning possible uses for eunuchs. He concludes by suggesting that all abbeys of religious women ought to be under the direction, not of a mother abbess, but of a father abbot. It is not hard to see what he was driving at. But here, for the first time, I should like to speak a word in Abélard's favor. There are easily twenty more tragic moments in his painful career, but none, I think, more profoundly moving. Who knows whether Héloïse herself, buried beneath her sorrow and still a prey to her devouring passion, really understood him?

How could Abélard, miserable as he was, have better demonstrated that very tenderness which Héloïse was to chide him for lacking than by doing what he had just done? All that remained to him in this world was the tiny parcel of land which some benefactor had given him, and this wretched oratory and a few cabins hastily built by his students. But the moment he heard that Héloïse was in need of shelter, he rushed from the ends of Brittany to give her the little he had. What a magnificent gesture! What a splendid token of deep and hidden affection now become beautiful and pure. It was in part the love of a noble priest for the deserted structure, once a church, and now once more to be restored to public worship. It was in part the charity of the Benedictine abbot for the homeless prioress and her daughters whom he was able to settle in a new home. But there was something more, too, and it ought to be said. There were other priests besides Abélard who might have been disturbed by this deserted oratory. There were other abbots than the Abbot of Saint-Gildas in a position to shelter this prioress and her religious. But it was not they, it was Abélard who did these things, and did them for Héloïse, because he was her husband and she was his wife. Himself a vagrant, hunted from place to place, Abélard dreamed for a passing instant of spending the rest of his life at the Paraclete near her whose life he had ruined, though it was she, rather, who daily accused herself of destroying his. He would have stayed there close to her, like a prudent friend, like a priest, like a father admiring her with all his soul and assisting her by his learning in the duties of the noble office to which she had just been raised. Exhausted by so much persecution at the hands of his brethren and sons, Abélard had hoped to find near his daughter "after the tumult and the tempest, a kind of haven and a little peace".[8]

But when things had reached this stage, calumny hunted him out again. What did he mean, he, the Abbot of Saint-Gildas, by not returning to his quarreling sons to whom duty, at least, bound him? Accordingly, he returned to his monastery, how we know not, but for reasons, as we shall see, known to Héloïse, even if she never accepted them. It was from Saint-Gildas that he actually wrote the *Historia calamitatum*. It was his most recent calamity, though neither the last nor the worst he was to undergo. He wrote this account of his own trials in order to console an afflicted and complaining friend. This long and painful complaint fell by chance into the hands of Héloïse—fortuitous circumstance to which we owe the first of her extant letters.

IV

The Ethics of Pure Love

IF WE accept as genuine those letters of Héloïse which have come down to us, it becomes possible to judge the affair no longer only from Abélard's point of view but from hers as well. For Abélard had personal reasons for wanting a secret marriage, while Héloïse, whose sentimental logic far surpassed Abélard's, had personal reasons for flatly opposing any kind of marriage. To her the whole plan seemed futile because she felt that nothing could ever calm Fulbert. Moreover, it seemed dangerous as well, and she dreaded the consequences of the equivocal position in which it would place the two of them. We have already seen why she considered the marriage to be dishonorable to Abélard. But she considered it so for herself too. The world might be unaware of her weakness, but she could hardly forget it herself. And just as she wanted Abélard to preserve a genuine personal honor, not merely the appearance of it, so was it her own personal honor with which she was deeply preoccupied. From the very moment she became his wife, Héloïse would never again be sure that she was not becoming an accomplice to Abélard's moral fall for the purpose of satisfying her personal interest. Such, in sum, was Hélo-

ïse's drama, and we can still follow its stormy course in the
letters which have been preserved. Not to lose ourselves in
the psychology of Héloïse, as the documents permit us to
understand it, we must realize at once that the evolution of
her passion followed a very different course from that of
Abélard. Abélard's case was a cold piece of calculation put
to the service of an unbridled sensuality; then he was overwhelmed by a violent passion for which he was willing to
degrade himself in his own eyes, and, since he had to preserve his reputation, to base his whole life on a lie. For
Héloïse, on the contrary, after a total surrender which
seems to have been made without a struggle, doubts and
scruples began to appear. There is no doubting their reality,
however; and since Héloïse herself out of a certain delicacy
remains silent about them, we depend for our information
on the rather tardy account of Abélard's remorse: "You
know how shamefully my passion had completely sacrificed our bodies. Respect neither for God nor decency,
even on those days when the Passion of Our Lord was being
so solemnly commemorated, deterred me from wallowing
in the mire. When you objected to it yourself and resisted
with all your might, and tried to dissuade me from it, I frequently forced your consent (for after all you were the
weaker) by threats and blows. I was bound to you by the
ardor of such desire that I forced these wretched pleasures
which we can no longer mention without shame before God
and myself."[1]

This tardy confession of Abélard's is of capital importance, not only because it attests the violence of his passion,
which alone accounts for the signal madness of the secret
marriage, but also, and above all, because it shows a side of

Héloïse which, without this unique text, we should never be able to guess. Until the moment of his mutilation, Abélard never allowed himself to be restrained by a scruple of any description. We must not belabor him needlessly, since he is confessing it himself. But how can we avoid contrasting with this unbridling of brutal sensuality, brutal to the point where it resorted to force, the scruples and hesitations of Héloïse? When one is aware of these things, the meaning of many other texts becomes vividly clear and opens new insights into the state of soul of the actors in this sad drama.

Although it is true, as we have seen, that Abélard and Héloïse had both admitted that the grand dignity of a philosopher and of a cleric was bound up with his continence and although they had admitted this for the same reasons, they did not both draw the same conclusions from it. Abélard concluded from this principle that he had to conceal his marriage, Héloïse that she ought not to marry. Abélard only acted out of vanity, considering only his reputation. But Héloïse, thinking always of Abélard's great dignity, only desired his personal glory. Héloïse's perfect honesty thus demanded not only that she refuse the marriage, but that she suggest a complete and final separation. Morally speaking, no other solution was possible, granting the nature of the problem and the terms in which the two lovers had stated it. Public or secret, Abélard's marriage degraded him in his own eyes and in those of Héloïse. While Abélard was quite willing to sacrifice his real honor as cleric and philosopher, provided its appearance remained to satisfy his vanity, Héloïse was ready to give up even the joys of passion from the moment the real reputation of Abélard demanded it. She was not satisfied that Abélard should have the air of greatness, she wanted him to be great. She wished this for his sake and for her own too, because her own grandeur was totally dependent upon that of the man she loved, and he could only injure himself in marrying her. Thence her direct arguments and the decisive conclusions she drew from them. By marriage Abélard was sanctioning forever a lapse that would otherwise be temporary. Unquestionably, once married, their love would become morally and religiously legitimate; but judged from the heights of the ideal of cleric and philosopher, their life would remain as impure as it was before, save that now it would be irrevocably confirmed in its impurity.

What lies at the basis of Héloïse's objections to every plan involving marriage is, primarily, the notion of the true personal glory of Abélard, which so often fired her with the courage to renounce him whom she loved, and which gave her at length the strength to propose a complete separation. But it was not merely from marriage that Héloïse hoped to turn her lover when she reminded him that the great philosophers gave up all pleasures so as to recognize no other tie than that of philosophy alone: "they denied themselves all sensual pleasures that they might repose in the arms of philosophy alone."[2] Héloïse, then, was far from regarding the marriage as reparation for their sin against the moral code. Rather she rejected it in terror as the absolute and perpetual sanction of their betrayal of their mutual ideal of what the true cleric and philosopher ought to be. As long as they were not married, Abélard could still regain his lost greatness because their separation was still possible. But if Héloïse was married to an Abélard who only married her out of carnal passion, she would never be able to protect him against himself, since she would have lost the right to refuse herself to him. The very thoughts of the fall threatening the man she loved for his personal greatness, and whose passion she was herself arousing to his eventual ruin, can alone give its full meaning to the last of her arguments, as Abélard reports it: "If therefore laymen and pagans have lived thus, without the restrictions of a religious profession, how much the more is it your duty to do so, you who are a cleric and a canon, lest you should come to prefer shameful pleasures to the divine service, lest you cast yourself into the gulf of Charybdis and perish, lest you should destroy yourself in these obscenities to the mockery of the whole world."[3] There is no mistaking the sense—"lest shamelessly and irrevocably you give yourself to these obscenities." Such "obscenities" are certainly inseparable from the married life, and a regular marriage could not make them legitimate for a cleric and philosopher of the stature of Abélard. It could only make them permanent by giving them, as it were, official sanction.

It has been necessary to insist on this point because it alone enables us to understand the strange situation in which Héloïse found herself when it became evident that nothing would ever dissuade Abélard from marrying her. She found herself, then, torn between two contradictory moral codes, the popular one which Abélard seemed quite prepared to accept and the code for heroes of the spiritual life which it was her duty not to allow him to abandon altogether; if possible, she had even to lead him back to its perfect practice. Abélard was ready to accept his fall. But Héloïse could not accept it either for herself or for him. When Abélard found that he could not get along without Héloïse,

to accept the marriage as a "remedy for concupiscence"
would have been a strict duty had it been a question of anyone else than a philosopher and cleric such as he. In his
case, however, the love of an Héloïse demanded heroic
moral principles, the only principles worthy of him or capable of keeping him worthy of her. Since Abélard was not
yet capable of tying himself down to continence, it was
necessary at least to avoid any commitment which would
forever deprive him of his liberty to return to it. What,
in brief, did Abélard want? He wanted Héloïse, not marriage. Since he could not do without her, Héloïse was going
to give in to him, but in yielding she hoped to delay his
ultimate collapse as much as possible in the hope of fore-
stalling it. Thus by a piece of sophistry comparable to
Abélard's, she suggested fornication rather than marriage.
While Abélard looked to marriage to appease his passion
and to preserve a semblance of glory, Héloïse refused marriage in order to preserve the very substance of this glory.
It is not for us to weigh the moral responsibilities in so profound a crisis. But let us at least say that since Abélard was
really incapable of remaining on the high level of the doc-
tors and scholars whose memory haunted him, he ought to
have acknowledged himself publicly for what he really
was, and not have insisted on the secrecy which only made
a lie of his life. But Héloïse, desperate as she was for love of
her hero whose greatness was hers too, was not helping him
to acknowledge himself for what he really was when she
offered to save his reputation at the price of his morality.
One hesitates to say this, but the passion for spiritual grandeur which is the secret source of their life story seems
never to have been completely pure. It was God's glory,

not their own that they should have considered in order to attain true greatness. But Abélard and Héloïse were never unmindful of themselves, and it is this which, in terms of the spiritual life, involved them more and more deeply in error. Abélard would hide his marriage so that the world would think him a Seneca or a St. Jerome. Héloïse suggested concubinage that once again he might become like these. The real tragedy of the action lies in the perfect sincerity with which they both played the comedy of sanctity.

But once Héloïse had chosen her role, she was woman enough to play it out perfectly to the bitter end. Speaking now for herself[4] and not for St. Jerome, she says that the title of lover will be far dearer to her and far more honorable than that of wife, for she wished only to hold Abélard by tenderness, not by the fetters of matrimony. She knew that it was sensuality that was driving Abélard towards marriage, and she wished to make him see that from this point of view all the advantages were in fornication: "If we separate for a time, our joys upon finding each other again will be far more pleasant because more seldom."[5] With inflexible logic, Héloïse now appealed to all that was base in Abélard to save him from a marriage that would tarnish his real splendor.

Abélard's apparent unconcern in thus divulging Héloïse's most intimate secrets might strike us as surprising, were we not perfectly sure that both of them saw nothing amiss in such an attitude. In fact, far from denying this text or reproaching Abélard for telling too much, Héloïse later accused him of having been too discreet in his presentation of this point. No doubt she saw in any understatement of the

case a diminution of her own glory and consequently of
Abélard's, because they were now one and the same thing.
Their glory was now that of a united pair, and the only
point on which they differed was the best manner of preserving it. Thus for Abélard's vague statement, "for these
reasons and others like them",[6] Héloïse makes the necessary
additions and precisions to remove all incertitude about the
true nature of her own intentions.

What justifies these revelations, from Héloïse's point of
view, is that although Abélard faithfully recorded her motives for opposing marriage, he passed over in almost complete silence her reasons for preferring "free love."[7] And
the two problems were totally distinct in her thought. Her
reasons for refusing the marriage, which she had borrowed
from St. Jerome, if accepted, could only have resulted in
their complete separation. But since Abélard persisted in
his folly: "since she was unable to turn aside my folly, and
since she was incapable of hurting me so deeply",[8] the problem now presented itself in an altogether new form. Since
Abélard had excluded once and for all the solutions calling
for a separation, it only remained to be seen whether Héloïse should be his in or outside of marriage. This was an
aspect of the problem which Abélard had not even thought
of, but which Héloïse felt obliged to solve, less for Abélard's honor than for her own.

Héloïse was quite certain that Abélard desired the marriage only to be assured of having her. On the other hand,
as she foresaw its effects, this marriage project seemed a
threat, perhaps to their lives, but certainly to Abélard's
glory. As she saw things, Abélard had nothing to gain from
the proposal and she had very much to lose by it. Indeed,

who did stand to gain by it in the eyes of public opinion? Fulbert perhaps, and above all Héloïse. But this was what she wished to avoid at any price. First of all, because it was false. Knowing, as she had firmly reminded him, that Abélard's true greatness demanded celibacy, she was quite ready, for her part, to make this sacrifice. But Abélard shrank from it. He wanted marriage and wanted it for his own sake. It was hardly just, then, that in the eyes of everyone she should be responsible for the marriage, when actually she had done everything in her power to dissuade him from it.

This, however, was not the least of Héloïse's objections. There was also the question of her love, that is, of everything she looked for in life; and this was about to be dishonored publicly by Abélard's wild project. In the moral misery in which she was plunged, Héloïse guarded only one thing of which she was proud, her love. It can be seen that she must have been intent on keeping it intact and allowing no equivocation to plane it down. It was all she had left truly worthy of respect. The marriage was going to compromise everything, because people would say that she had allowed herself to be seduced by Abélard in order to be able to marry him. Unable to prevent Abélard from irrevocably confirming his own fall, Héloïse begged him at least not to make her do the same. If it was necessary, she would be his mistress, and then, be it for well or ill, no one at least could accuse her of having sold what she wished to give.

Hence that justly famous passage in which the Abbess of the Paraclete called God to witness that she preferred to belong to Abélard in free love rather than in the married state; that even if Augustus, the ruler of the whole world,

did her the honor of asking her to marry him and to share
with him his imperial sway, she would deem it sweeter and
more worthy to be the mistress of Abélard than wife of the
Emperor.[9] The fact that Héloïse should freely have uttered a statement like this when the question could no
longer arise for her, and when her religious dignity invited
her to leave it alone, proves well enough that her feelings
had up to this time lost none of their force nor altered
in character. She spoke in the present. She believed her
position unchanged. She would have done it again if she
had had to. Even as she was writing, arguments came tum-
bling one after the other to justify a course of action which
she would never disavow. Certainly all these arguments
amounted to the same thing: "God knows I never wanted
anything from you but yourself—*te pure, non tua, con-
cupiscens*. It was not marriage, no, nor gain of any kind
that I was looking for; it was not my own desires nor my
own pleasures, but yours, as you very well know, that I
longed to satisfy. No doubt the name of wife is stronger
and more sacred, but I have always preferred that of mistress, or, if you will pardon me for saying it, concubine and
prostitute. For the more I degraded myself for you, the
more did I hope to find favor with you. Besides, in humiliating myself thus, I was not wounding the splendor of
your glory."[10] The very essence of this total love, that
which, for Héloïse, constituted its true grandeur, and the
only thing indeed that really mattered to her, was its complete and absolute disinterestedness. "I have kept nothing
for myself" *(Nihil mihi reservavi)*. Here is the very basis
of her life; and not a single line she ever wrote suggests
anything to the contrary.

Although these surprising sentiments were very much
Héloïse's own, they were derived, probably through Abélard, from the writings of Cicero. The notion of the essentially disinterested nature of friendship presented in the
De amicitia vividly impressed writers of the twelfth century. Cicero had convinced them that the fruit of true love
was to be found in the love itself: "all the enjoyment of
love is in the love itself."[11] This thesis had deeply impressed
Bernard of Clairvaux.[12] And Abélard several times quotes
Cicero on this subject. How important he regarded this
doctrine can be seen in the way he uses it in his Commentary on the Epistle to the Romans,[13] and also in the poetic
Advice to Astrolabe where a relatively long passage deals
with pure friendship in a manner quite Ciceronian.[14] A
comparison of this text with Cicero's dialogue will establish
their relationship. Abélard's only notable modification of
his master's doctrine is the indulgent view he takes of those
who do evil to please a friend. He accepts Cicero's principle, but at the same time manages to find excuses for the
guilty party. "To bow to the will of a friend who makes a
dishonest request is to stray from the true path of friendship. However, he whose entreaties force the other to act
sins more gravely than he who, overcome by the other's
prayers, only reluctantly consents"!

Although we cannot be sure of it, still it is probable that
Abélard was thinking of Héloïse when he wrote these lines.
No doubt he hoped himself to bear the brunt of the accusation which their son might one day make. Whatever may
be the case, the fact remains that Héloïse's flight from marriage in so far as it arises from the demands of pure love
comes from the De amicitia. She accepts its doctrine on this

point. It is very difficult to say whether it was Héloïse or Abélard who won the other over to these principles which they both ultimately held. It may well have been Abélard who first taught them to Héloïse, but certainly it was she alone who really knew how to practice them.

Once her thinking took this course, Héloïse found herself on an endless road of moral casuistry where all the accepted values were to undergo a radical transformation. Deaf to all her objurgations, Abélard had continued to urge the marriage, and he finally got his way. For Héloïse, the decision spelled their ruin, since Abélard was losing thereby his personal honor as she was losing hers, he in placing himself beyond the state of continency, she as accessory to the act. At the same time, she was giving her own disinterested love every appearance of a callous piece of calculation. Héloïse felt that in marrying Abélard she was guilty of a crime—indeed of the only crime for which she could never forgive herself.

Let there be no mistake about it. Héloïse never totally condemned herself for being Abélard's mistress. No doubt she knew as well as anybody, and better than most, that fornication was a serious sin. She did her best, accordingly, to be sorry for it. But how could she ever fully repent a weakness she never ceased to desire? What she could do, however, and never ceased doing was to blame herself for ever marrying Abélard at all. This indiscretion she repented bitterly. In giving her consent to this marriage, she had sinned against Abélard's glory, had allowed him to place himself in the false position which no doubt precipitated Fulbert's vengeance. If Héloïse posed for herself any moral problem, if there is anything she turned over and over to examine from all possible angles, it is rather her sin against Abélard than her sin against God. From her reflections on this theme there arose in her those temptations to rebel which later forced Abélard to remind her of the respect due to her new state in life.

Each time Héloïse returned to this perplexing problem, two conflicting judgments troubled her mind: she was guilty, yet at the same time she was innocent. Guilty of contributing to Abélard's downfall, she could at least console herself that she had never wished him anything but good. If she had greatly injured him, it was with a great innocence: "If I am hurting you exceedingly, I am, as you know, exceedingly innocent" (*et plurimum nocens, plurimum, ut nosti, sum innocens*).[15]

Caught between these conflicting certainties, Héloïse had naturally to seek to reassure herself of her own innocence, and this she achieved by combining two fundamental notions, for both of which she was probably indebted to Abélard. In any case, they form a part of the ethics and theology of both. One of these notions we already know, the doctrine of pure love; the other is the morality of intention which Abélard has developed systematically in his *Scito te ipsum*. Their synthesis and application to her own case is the work of Héloïse herself. If her love is pure of all interest in that it only seeks its recompense in itself, it is justified, as by definition; and since it is the intention alone which determines the moral value of the act, every act, even one guilty in itself, if it is dictated by a sentiment of pure love, will be by the same token innocent.

This rather surprising doctrine supposes that an act can be culpable yet legitimate at one and the same time. But this is precisely what Héloïse needed to consider herself as being at the same time *nocens* (inflicting injury) and *innocens* (guiltless). Abélard's theology provided her with all the arguments required to justify her attitude. According to the *Scito te ipsum*, the good or bad quality of the act resides entirely in the intention which inspires it. Abélard pushes this thesis to the extent of saying that the external part of a sin renders it in no way more culpable or blameworthy in the eyes of God.[16] To sin is one thing, the external accomplishment of the sin is another, and the first can exist in its entirety without the second.[17] A good intention is one thing, a good act another. Since it is here a question of two radically distinct goods, each of which is sufficient to itself, it is impossible to add one to the other. The good act adds nothing, therefore, to the good intention.[18] This complete separation of intentions and acts renders possible and even inevitable the occurrence of mixed cases in which the moral quality of the act may be contrary to that of the intention. The executioners who persecuted the martyrs or crucified Christ were not guilty of sin by these acts if they judged that it was their duty to do them.[19] Thus one can perform a materially culpable act with a good intention or a materially culpable act with a bad intention. Indeed, the act itself matters little, since in the eyes of God the intention alone counts.[20] The act itself is not taken into consideration in His judgment.[21] The act would count for something with God if anything could hurt Him. If the intention alone counts, it is because one cannot hurt God, but only scorn Him.[22]

This doctrine of Abélard forms all the armor of the system of autojustification imagined by Héloïse. She recalls

first of all that what counts in these matters is not what we do but the interior dispositions with which we do them: "In a wicked deed, rectitude of action depends not on the effect of the thing but on the affections of the agent, not on what is done but with what dispositions it is done."[23] This is why we see her afterwards furiously take up her cudgels, this time without the least pity for Abélard, to show him, in order to convince herself, the perfect purity of her love for him. It was as though her very salvation depended upon her success or failure in establishing this point. Abélard's was the only testimony to these sentiments which Héloïse would accept. He alone could vouch for them, as he alone was their object. For Abélard, God was the judge who probes loins and hearts; but for Héloïse it was Abélard who played this role, though the judge sometimes found himself in the prisoner's dock.

Thus we find her, on another occasion, trying to show the purity and disinterestedness of her love by contrasting it with Abélard's. She was for the moment indignant with him because he was leaving her to herself. She was a little jealous, too, because he had written the story of his calamities for someone else and had never written anything for her. She still loved him as much or more than ever, although they had been separated by the misfortune which had overtaken Abélard. The heart of the Abbess of the Paraclete had remained unchanged from the day she had become Abélard's lover. Nothing in her had altered. This she felt, not without some naïveté, was the decisive experience. From the fact that she still loved him as much as ever, and in the same manner, even though she could expect nothing from him either as mistress or as wife, Héloïse concluded

that at the time when she was his mistress, and later too as
his wife, she had already loved him without expecting anything from him.

On this point we must be as precise as she was. It is
rather surprising that she felt the need of pushing the thesis
so far. To suppose that she sought her own pleasure even
once in her love of Abélard would be to deny that her love
was pure and would destroy the very basis of her self-
justification. Let us repeat with her: "I sought not my own
pleasure but yours".[24] And the proof—that she still loved
Abélard even after such pleasures became quite impossible.
He, on the contrary, no longer loved her because he had
to forgo the pleasures. Thus, he never really loved her. It
had been concupiscence which had bound him to Héloïse,
not "friendship" in the Ciceronian sense, not disinterested
tenderness existing for its own sake. "Concupiscence rather
than friendship bound you to me, the ardor of desire rather
than love". The sentiments of love which Abélard professed to experience vanished the moment he could no
longer have what he wanted. With a severity most unusual
in her, Héloïse concluded her indictment thus: "This is
no personal judgment, my beloved, it is the judgment of
everyone. It is not just my own, everyone is saying it. It
is no private opinion; it is public opinion. I wish I were
alone in thinking so, because if anyone could justify you,
it would relieve my sorrow. If I could even manufacture
excuses for you, I should be better able to conceal my own
dejection."[25] An understandable bitterness, certainly! For
if Héloïse was wrong about Abélard, how could she ever
be consoled for her sacrifice? But these reproaches were

not entirely just, because Abélard had not completely for-saken Héloïse. Nor were they without a certain naïveté because Abélard's positions before and after the mutilation are scarcely comparable. She still retained certain feelings which were wanting in him.

Whatever may be the case here, the essential thing for us is that Héloïse thought she was justified in presenting this testimony. It was her profound conviction that her love was totally unselfish, even in its sensual aspects, which was the basis of her self-justification. Whether we are shocked by it or not, the insistence with which the Abbess of the Paraclete reminds us that she was ready to endure every sort of shame rather than marry Abélard, can be ex-plained in no other way. At this period of her life, she had no intention of rebelling against moral and religious law. She very well knew that such a course of action would have been a violation of these, and that such a violation would have been gravely culpable. But this was not the question at stake. When she married Abélard, she became the cause of the crime committed against him. In her, the old prin-ciple that woman is man's downfall again found its verifica-tion. Because of Eve, Adam was driven from his earthly paradise. Delilah delivered Samson to his enemies and so caused him, after he was blinded, to bury himself under the ruins of the Temple. Again, women made a fool of the great King Solomon and caused him to offer sacrifice to Astarte. It was Job's wife who tried him to make him blas-pheme in his misfortune; and it was against her he had his harshest struggle The devil knows well that the woman is always a ready-made cause of man's destruction. This is how, by setting for him the trap of Héloïse, he succeeded in destroying Abélard by marriage where he had failed to destroy him by fornication.

When Héloïse consented to marry Abélard, she became an accomplice of the devil in this catastrophic plot. Hence she was guilty even before the marriage when she yielded to the attractions of the flesh and lived in a continual state of sin. It was these earlier sins which led Abélard to insist on marrying her. No doubt it was in punishment for them that she was doomed to consent to the marriage. Nevertheless, and it was to this profound conviction that she was so passionately attached, she never actually accepted the marriage, even though she had to submit to it. This is why, at a distance of twelve or fifteen years from the events, she maintained with fierce obstinacy that she would still be ready, if necessary, to prostitute herself for him if by this means she could turn him from so wild a project. Like so many women before her, she had become the instrument of ruin for the man she loved. She had committed a crime, but she had never consented to it. This is why in the last analysis she is innocent. When Delilah destroyed Samson, she wanted to do so. But when the subtle Tempter of men used Héloïse to destroy Abélard by forcing her into the fatal marriage, he had indeed made her commit the fault but he had not succeeded in making her consent to it. "He did not draw me into sin with my consent as he did the women mentioned above."[26] Now, as we know, it is consent alone which constitutes the sin. The exterior act itself does not change the nature of the intention which dictated it. Héloïse, therefore, is innocent of the crime which she has committed. Her case has been proved.

We recognize here their mutual theology. In using such theology, Héloïse became the first of many romantic heroines driven into evil by love—"it was through love that the subtle Tempter turned me to evil ways" *(quam tamen in causam commissae malitiae ex affectu convertit)*—but exonerated from blame because their love was pure. They are led to commit sins but remain innocent even in committing them. Their appeal is to a system of ethics which separates the order of acts from the order of intentions. How can I be guilty, Rousseau will reiterate incessantly, since my conscience reproaches me with nothing? It is hardly by chance that his Julie d'Étanges was for him a new Héloïse. What is really surprising is how the old Héloïse went so much farther than the new along the treacherous path in which she preceded her. For Julie d'Étanges spent a lifetime of tears in expiation for a sin against a moral code. But Héloïse's tears were not in expiation for a sin against a moral code. On this score, she found herself completely innocent. The sin she had committed was against Abélard.

V

The Conversion of Abélard

WHILE Héloïse was carrying on the harsh struggle which her letters describe, Abélard was conducting his own with equal heroism but in an altogether different spirit. We know well enough his reason for entering religion. There is no reason to suppose that he would ever have been a monk save for the misfortune that covered him with shame in the eyes of all. Unlike Héloïse, however, he never said that a vocation to the monastic way of life played no part in his decision to become a monk. Rather to the contrary, the complex motives behind the decision give a sufficiently large place to a purely religious sentiment, that there can be no mistaking the true reasons for his entrance into religion. Héloïse went into the monastery in passionate obedience to Abélard's orders. More than twelve years later the Abbess of the Paraclete still did not accept unreservedly the blow which God had struck her. With Abélard it was different. He accepted at once and completely the cruel form of expiation which God imposed upon him. Certainly he wept over his lost glory and lamented his departed honor. But the sentiments he experienced at this time included also the desire to accept the divine will and to expiate his sin against God and against Fulbert. There is no reason to doubt the reality of either of these. "By a just judgment of God, I was punished in the part of my body with which I had sinned. By a just betrayal, he whom I had myself betrayed, paid me back in kind."[1] It is comparatively easy to find men accepting the judgment of God. But if Abélard could thus publicly acknowledge his sin against Fulbert, who had always struck him as hateful and ridiculous, his conscience must genuinely have recognized the justice of the punishment which overtook him. Let us accept his testimony at its face value. Shame before the world was a stronger motive for entering religion than the desire to consecrate himself to God.[2] Nevertheless, the one motive did not exclude the other; and his total submission to God's judgment, in contrast with Héloïse's stubborn rebellion, seems to have been the germ of his whole religious life, the starting point and support of his soul's spiritual growth.

We don't know just when Abélard became a priest. He says nothing himself on this subject. But it is certain that he received the priesthood, because Héloïse thereafter no longer addressed him as "you, cleric and canon", but as "you, monk and priest".[3] We know that he was already a priest when he became Abbot of Saint-Gildas, because he complained that someone had put poison in his chalice in order to get rid of him.[4] He must even have been a priest during his retreat at the Paraclete when he was in hiding in this solitude with his assisting cleric,[5] and was the only minister in the Oratory of the Holy Trinity. We are thus led to believe that he was ordained priest shortly after becoming a monk. Whatever the actual facts, we are reasonably sure that as soon as he assumed these two new titles, he took

them seriously and endeavored to turn them to account
with as complete an absence of scruples as if he had received
them in the usual way. Once a monk, Abélard went the
whole way. He was more a monk than any other monk.
He was a monk in the only manner he could be anything—
without compromise, without measure, with the fierce en-
ergy of a will struggling against despair.

This complete giving of himself brought a new series of
misfortunes upon him. God, it seems, had struck him but
to deliver him from the thorn of his flesh and to free him
for the works of the spirit. Thus, when Abélard found
himself restored by force to a position of dignity from
which he ought never to have fallen, he was determined to
tolerate no such lapse in others. He began with trying to
reform the ways of the monks of Saint-Denys, including
those of the abbot whose life he tells us was as abject and
infamous as his position was exalted. Because he reproved
them often and vehemently both in private and public, he
soon became absolutely unbearable and hateful to everyone: "I made myself exceedingly troublesome and odious
to all."[6] Since these first results failed to satisfy him, he
undertook to demonstrate to a canon regular that the state
of the monk surpassed in dignity not only the cleric's but
even that of the priest and bishop. Why does the Church in
her Litanies invoke "All ye holy monks and hermits" rather
than "All ye holy clerics, priests and bishops"? Clearly because the state of religious perfection proper to the monastic
life surpasses the highest dignities of the secular clergy by
as much as the contemplative life surpasses the active life!
Abélard calls upon St. Jerome, Seneca, Cicero, one after
the other, to support his thesis. This, of course, is all per-

fectly true. But we are a little surprised that this violent protagonist of monastic purity so completely forgot how easy it had become for him, and at how little cost he could now share the glory of this perfection.[7] Such uncompromising zeal for the religious ideal in a monk whose own vocation was suspect, was certainly not likely to win him sympathy. As we look back at these events over the intervening centuries, we are tempted to smile and wonder at it all; and it is only Abélard's complete guilelessness and sincerity which restrains us. Once a monk, Abélard gave himself completely to God.[8]

Abélard had other possible choices after the vicious assault on his person. No matter how crushing the shame of the moment, there was no reason why he could not have waited a little while and then returned to his teaching. His reputation as cleric, philosopher, and theologian would be above suspicion, and perhaps not even seriously diminished. Or if he preferred to enter religion, he was under no obligation to reform the monasteries in which he happened to be living, either Saint-Denys or, later, Saint-Gildas. Even supposing he could not himself be reconciled to a partial observance of the rule, he could at least have bound only himself to the strict observance and given the monastery the example of a perfect Benedictine, without restoring on the borders of Ardusson the austerities of the Fathers of the Desert.[9] But Abélard had no use for half-measures. If he was to become a teaching monk, his model was close at hand—Origen, "the greatest Christian philosopher", whose pre-eminence held no terrors for him. Both Abélard and Origen, thanks to their mutilation, voluntary or forced, were delivered from the passions of the flesh. Like Origen,

Abélard was an illustrious philosopher; like Origen, too, Abélard was a born theologian. Certain of both these facts, Abélard wanted to transform himself from the philosopher of the world, which he had been, into the philosopher of God. In the desire to win souls to the study of the only true philosophy, Sacred Scripture, he wanted to busy himself with those rash speculations which were to bring him from the Council of Soissons to the Council of Sens. To imitate Origen, however, was no easy matter. But for a will straining after greatness, the risk was worth running. Abélard was confident that he could avoid further shipwreck. In any case, he preferred to be nothing at all than to fall short of true greatness. What he had always wished to be as a theologian, he now wished to be as a monk. Indeed, these two great disciplines are inseparably linked with true Christian grandeur, sanctity. Abélard simply had to seek it because it was the highest perfection. Everything indicates that this is what he was after. Not the least of the many surprises for Héloïse, religious for the love of Abélard, was to encounter an Abélard so different from the one she had known. Totally bent on loving God, he had bowed before the transforming *conversio* of religious profession. He was now about to outstrip Héloïse in the way of divine love as she had once excelled him in the perfection of human love.

From this moment, Abélard continued to grow in mental and spiritual stature. Indeed, in the past he had not been quite so great a philosopher as people would have him think, nor so great a theologian as he himself thought. But he was now to become a great enough Christian to satisfy at the same time St. Bernard of Clairvaux and Peter the Venerable, in itself no mean achievement. But it is only just to add that Abélard not only strove himself for Christian perfection, but did all he could to have Héloïse do the same. If the collection of letters preserved for us forms a whole and presents so remarkable a unity, if either Abélard or Héloïse, or both of them together, wanted this one fragment of their correspondence transmitted to posterity, it is because it relates their true feelings at one of the most critical points of their history. It was here that Abélard realized to his horror that the Abbess of the Paraclete was the same Héloïse he had known in the world. All his endeavors were henceforth directed towards obtaining from this exemplary religious the *conversio* which she was rejecting, or at least thought she was rejecting. God alone knows whether he ever obtained it, granted, of course, that it was really wanting. These letters which tell all, leave us struggling with the secret of two interior lives, too deep even to understand themselves. But this time it was Abélard who was master and guide. Let us, then, like Héloïse, follow him as well as we can.

In order to give this part of their correspondence the same sense it had in their eyes and which, as far as they were concerned, justified its publication, it is once more necessary to turn to St. Jerome. The letters Héloïse was seeking from Abélard were of a very definite kind. She wanted the kind of letters or treatises of instruction, exhortation, and consolation which some of the Church Fathers had upon occasion written for holy women.[10] Abélard knew very well what she wanted. It is just possible that he had not written Héloïse since their entering religion. But we know nothing at all about this, nor is it necessarily implied by his reply to Héloïse's first letter. "Since our entrance into religion I have not yet written you any words of consolation or of exhortation"[11] only means: "I have not yet written for you such letters of spiritual direction as Jerome once wrote for the illustrious virgins and widows whose consciences he was directing." In brief, a new Marcella was awaiting her St. Jerome.[12] Abélard had no right to refuse.

Indeed, he seems never to have dreamed of refusing her. To appreciate fully what Abélard was undertaking for Héloïse, it is not enough merely to recall the various letters he wrote for her on special occasions, even if this includes the veritable treatise he composed for her on the religious rule. The *Epistola de studio litterarum*, the *Heloissae problemata*, his *Hexameron*, the hymns and sequences composed at her request, the collection of sermons preached to the religious of the Paraclete which, contrary to his usual practice, he prepared expressly for them,[13] abundantly witness his lively sense of spiritual responsibility at the time. The most surprising thing is not that he undertook to write the letters. Indeed, he seems not even to have hesitated about this. What is really surprising is that for once he was completely successful. There are many limitations in his work on logic, still more in his theology. But if one is looking for a work of Abélard without any limitations, an undertaking in which he shows himself more than equal to his task, it is to be found in these Letters to Héloïse. Certainly, the human pathos of Heloïse is still more touching. Even where he is right, Abélard cannot take the leading role, dramatically speaking, from the woman who loves him, whom he has lost forever, and from whom it is his cruel duty to wrest consent to the sacrifice which he has himself imposed. But when all is said and done, this time it is Abélard who is right. He is only asking of Héloïse what she both can and should give him.[14]

This side of Abélard is so completely obscured by the controversies of the logician and theologian that it is necessary, even while apologizing for saying such simple things, to recall at what point his attitude towards Héloïse became that of a brother, a father, and a Christian.

Right from the beginning of his reply, Abélard sounds the true note which he never afterwards loses: "To Héloïse, his dearly beloved sister in Christ, Abélard, her brother in Him. . . . Sister, once so dear to me in the world, now exceedingly dear to me in Christ."[15] When Héloïse obstinately reminds him that she is his wife and that her passion for him is not yet dead, Abélard unwearyingly replies that the love he now bears her, like that which she should henceforth bear him, though no less ardent than the former, is and must be of a totally different kind. "To her only one after Christ, she who is his only one in Christ", writes Héloïse; "To the spouse of Christ from the servant of Christ", replies Abélard. It is unjust to accuse him here of coldness or indifference, because he is saying precisely what he should say—that Héloïse is still his wife but the Abbess of Paraclete is the spouse of Christ. We can only admire her clever retort: "To God, in species, but to Abélard as individual"! What a logician! Abélard himself could get no further with her, so we too must perforce be content. Since Héloïse, however, was availing herself of the privileges of the virgin Eustochium, Abélard had the right to quote in reply the words of St. Jerome: "I address you as *Madame*, Eustoch-

ium, for I must address as *Ma Dame* the spouse of my Lord
(*dominam quippe debeo vocare sponsam Domini mei*)."
Spouse of the Lord, Héloïse was now too highly enthroned
for Abélard to think he could honor her by calling her his
wife. What greater praise than that she who was once the
wife of a mere man should be called now the spouse of the
sovereign king?[16]

We must not imagine that we are here dealing with hol-
low figures of speech. As Abélard develops them, he finds
tones which no rhetoric could inspire. Those pages where
he describes for Héloïse all the scenes of the Passion of
Our Lord are as beautiful as the most inspired pages of St.
Bernard! And he writes them that they may touch her
heart! If it is pure love she seeks, where will she find truer
than in Christ who died on the cross to save her? Shrewdly
and eloquently, Abélard turns back on Héloïse one after
the other the arguments with which she had confronted
him. If it is disinterested love she is looking for, and if she
thinks she can find it nowhere save in herself, why does she
not turn towards the Creator of the world who, though He
sought nothing from her nor from anyone, sought for love
of her the most frightful torments? It is you, Héloïse wrote
to Abélard, not your goods that I loved. And what more,
he replies, does God seek in you than yourself? He is your
true friend, for it is you He is seeking, not what you possess.
Héloïse accuses Abélard of having never loved her sincerely. True, he replies, and reason enough that she should
turn from him to God, who alone has truly loved her; "My
love, which involved us both in sin, let us not call it love
but concupiscence. In you I cloyed a wretched appetite,
which was all I really loved." When Héloïse refers to all

that Abélard has suffered for her, he replies that it was not for her but by her and in his own despite; whereas, on the contrary, God had willingly sacrificed Himself for her. How unjust of her, then, to weep for Abélard's pains justly incurred, rather than for the iniquitous torment of an innocent God![17]

To challenge Héloïse thus to pure love was a master stroke on Abelard's part, and he was able to do it without abandoning the safe ground of abstract generalities. On the other hand, when replying to what he called Héloïse's perpetual revenge on God,[18] Abélard could hardly avoid the most shattering personal analysis. He brought her to task with a vigor that some have found shocking but which, we must concede, Héloïse's whole attitude made necessary. The Abbess of the Paraclete was not only refusing to accept God's punishment; she was accusing her judge. How unforgettable that cry of hers, worthy of Racine's Phèdre, "O God, if one dare say it, cruel art Thou to me in everything!"[19] Héloïse's complaints against God were many and precise. He had made her the most famous and happiest of women, only to prepare for her a hard fall. He had spared the two of them so long as they lived in fornication, only to strike them down when their love became legitimate and their life chaste; when, lawfully married, they lived, one in Paris, the other in Argenteuil. And finally, a last complaint where we find the vengeful power of feminine logic, ever infinite in its own right, fending desperately for survival: since God wanted to punish them in spite of everything, why had He struck only Abélard who had already done reparation even to the extent of stooping to marry Héloïse?[20]

This rebellion could not fail to frighten Abélard, for if he was not ignorant of the fact that Héloïse might at one time have nursed such sentiments, he thought at least that she had long since renounced them. But, as we see, such was not the case. She was leading a double life. She was pretending to be at the same time the passionate lover of yore and the abbess of a Benedictine convent. What is more, she was pretending to lead an irreproachable monastic life while stubbornly refusing to accept its religious motives. As Abélard roundly told her, Héloïse could not persist in such an attitude without destroying herself body and soul.[21] But with her inflexible will, it was no easy matter to make her yield, and, if one finds Abélard guilty of a certain roughness, it is well to remember that he was faced with a difficult task. After all, even in resorting to strong measures, he never got Héloïse to disavow the sentiments she had just expressed. Abélard's only hope was in the fact that these sentiments were not all from the same source nor of the same quality. When Héloïse writes: "I am still young and full of life; I love you more than ever and suffer bitterly from living a life for which I have no vocation," she is describing with heart-rending simplicity the most tragic of all conceivable situations. "The pleasures of lovers which we have tasted together have been so sweet that I cannot despise them nor even efface their memory without great difficulty. Wherever I turn, there they confront me with their eternal longing. Even in my sleep, their shadows pursue me. It is not until the time of Mass, when prayer should be purest, that the obscene imagining of these pleasures so completely overwhelms my poor soul that I yield to their shameful delectation rather than to prayer. I who should tremble at what I have done, sigh after what I have lost. Nor is it only what we have done but the very places, the moments which we have been together that are so deeply graven into my heart that once more I see them with you in all their plenitude. I cannot escape from them even in my sleep. Sometimes the very movements of my body show forth the thoughts of my soul, betraying themselves in involuntary words. How unhappy I am! Well may I recite the complaint of the soul in pain: 'Pitiable creature that I am, who is to deliver me from this body of death?' "[22]

There is no mistaking these accents, and, as we shall see, Abélard has taken care not to reply ironically on this point. But Héloïse maintains other positions much less sound from which Abélard might hope to dislodge her. He wondered, and every reader of the letters of Héloïse wonders with him, whether they did not express, over and above a profound and sincere distress, a kind of voluntary stubbornness, a sort of hardening into a pose once spontaneous enough but which now she wanted to preserve at any price. In brief, it is not impossible that Héloïse may have wished to play a role something like that which Pompey attributed to Cornelia: "This is your opportunity for undying fame. Your sex must win renown not in government or in war but only in a husband's misfortune."[23] If this was all that was left her to glory in, why not at least exploit it?

Thus, in Héloïse we seem to find something of that deliberate nursing of grief which Lucan noted in Cornelia: "She clasps closely the sorrow which consumes her; finds joy in her tears and loves her grief in place of her husband."[24] A sorrow thus cultivated is no less cruel, but there is an admixture of artifice in the means maintaining it and a consequent loss of sincerity of expression.

In Héloïse's case, the artifice was much more difficult to conceal because the sorrow concerned was so authentic and it was so completely discordant in the religious life she professed. This is why Héloïse, however touching her plight must always seem, has not the finer role in this duel with Abélard. From now on, it is he who is in the right and she in the wrong. Abélard realizes this and abuses, perhaps, his advantage. But it was a question of Héloïse's salvation in both this world and the next. So long as there remained any hope that she was not incorrigible, he felt obliged to use every means to help her.

Héloïse, we remember, had made the *Historia calamitatum* the occasion to demand vigorously either Abélard's physical presence at the Paraclete or letters of spiritual direction and occasional news about him. Abélard realized that he had never written a single letter of consolation or exhortation after their entry into religion and sought to excuse himself by claiming that the wonderful prudence and competence of Héloïse rendered his counsels unnecessary. He promised, however, to reply to all questions of this nature that the sisters might like to ask him.[25] Again, since Héloïse had expressed uneasiness about his lot in general, Abélard replies very simply that the best way of protecting him against the perils threatening him daily is to pray for him. There is nothing more powerful with God than the prayers of women for those who are dear to them. Let Héloïse then pray for him. To this end he sent her a psalter.[26] If her prayers were not enough, there were al-

ways those of the holy virgins and widows living with her
to obtain for him the protection he needed.[27] But why, indeed, should not her prayers suffice? How could they be
anything but acceptable in the eyes of God?[28] When he
was living near the religious of the Paraclete, they added to
the daily recitation of their Hours special prayers for Abélard. Then reminding her of the actual text of the prayers
they were saying for him when present, he sent others to
be said when he was absent.[29] What more could they do for
him? In truth, nothing save perchance, in the event of his
natural or violent death, to seek out his body wherever it
might be buried or exposed and bring it back to their own
cemetery. Then, whenever they look at his tomb his daughters, or rather his sisters, in Christ will remember to say a
prayer for him. Could any spot be more fitting for Christian burial than the abode of the servants of Christ? These
were Abélard's last requests. He concluded with the sup-
plication that the religious of the Paraclete show later on
for the welfare of his soul some of their present excessive
care for the welfare of his body.[30] Abélard's whole letter
has a correctness of tone that is truly perfect. Héloïse had
put forward her rights over him as her spouse. He asks her
rather to exercise her rights as spouse of Christ. She had
asked him for counsel; he promises it. She had spoken of
her passion for him; he asks her to pray passionately to God
that His grace may keep them safe. She begged him to return to the Paraclete; he asks that the sisters at least bring
back his body after his death. Everywhere the human sentiments of Héloïse are raised to the level of the divine in terms
both firm and discreet.

Abélard's suggestions appear to have been futile; and he

no doubt experienced some irritation at the surprising re-
action of Héloïse. He had asked his daughters not to forget
to pray for him after his death. And Héloïse's reply? After
your death! As though we could survive you! You will
have to celebrate our funeral rites and convey us first to the
hands of God. How could we pray to God for you when
we should be busy reproaching Him for your death? They
will have to bury us together, so how will we be able to
bury you? It is to be hoped, in this case, that the daughters
of Abélard precede him to the grave rather than follow him.
Let him never again speak to them about his death. The
very idea so upsets them that they become quite incapable
even of saying the Office which he has prescribed! Certainly, death is inevitable, but why think about it in advance? As Seneca says: "It is to walk ahead of evil and to
lose one's life even before death." Let us rather pray to God
in the words which Lucan, in his wisdom, addressed to
God:

> May whatever you prepare come without warning!
> Let the mind of men be blind to future destiny!
> May he who fears, at least have hope![31]

Héloïse hardly expected us to believe that if Abélard died
the whole convent of the Paraclete would die too and be
interred with him. Her words must, then, be some kind of
conventional formula.[32] What's more, far from counseling
her daughters to meditate on the last things, this mother
abbess was demanding that God grant Abélard the grace
of a sudden death. Truly this is more like the Stoicism of
Seneca and Lucan than the Christianity she professed. Abé-

lard must have been somewhat annoyed by it all and the logician in him no doubt longed to restore her to some semblance of coherence. She had asked him to give her some account of his misfortunes. He answered that he was in danger of death. She replied in her turn that he must never speak of such things. Does this mean, says Abélard, that when you ask news of me you only want to hear good news? If you prefer not to know the dangers threatening me, why ask me to speak about them? And when I regard death as a welcome deliverance from the frightful life I lead, why do you refuse to consider it in the same light?

From this point on, argument after argument comes from Abélard's pen as he strives to dislodge Héloïse from her position. Does she accuse herself of an unworthiness which renders her prayers futile? Could this unreasonable self-abasement of Héloïse's be a kind of coquettishness? She humiliates herself to be exalted, and like Galatea "hides in the willows, carefully showing the place."[33] Moreover, if it is rebellion against God's will which makes her unworthy of penitence, why not at least yield to Abélard's will which enjoins her to renounce rebellion? Héloïse boasts that she is ready to follow him even to hell. Can it be that the only place where she will not follow him is heaven?[34] Whereupon, resolutely applying the iron to the wound, Abélard tries furiously to make her see how grave have been their faults and how salutary the divine punishment. And as far as their separation after marriage was concerned, during which God saw fit to strike them, was it, asks Abélard with heartless precision, as chaste as Héloïse pretended? Why, the very respect due to a place consecrated to the Virgin had not been able to check their impurities. To say nothing of their previous sins, this alone was enough to justify their chastisement.[35] A salutary chastisement, moreover, and a justice tempered with mercy, because Abélard was now circumcised in soul as in body, liberated like Origen, without committing the crime by which Origen paid for his liberation.[36] But what can we say for Héloïse?

There is nothing in all the works of Abélard quite comparable with the burning, urgent pages in which the Abbot of Saint-Gildas tries desperately to get Héloïse to renounce her self-will. God has destined her for Himself from all eternity, for He calls Himself Heloim and has named her Héloïse. The marriage which she curses, God has willed for them because Abélard owes to it the mutilation which delivered him from his sins and because Héloïse, bound as she now was to Abélard, owes to it her forced renunciation of the world and her giving of herself to God. The family which she would have raised in the world, she now bears spiritually in the cloister. Saved as she is from the cesspool of the world, does she not live a life more worthy of herself in meditation, study, and prayer than that she would have led in the world? The sacred hands of Héloïse, fashioned for turning the pages of holy saints' lives, ought not be profaned by the vulgar labor of ordinary women. And if it is pure love she seeks, where indeed will she find a purer than that of Christ, her true spouse? What she said herself about Abélard's never having truly loved her is, alas, only too true. He never loved her for herself but coveted her for himself. But Christ, on the other hand, loved Héloïse for herself when He suffered a most ignominious and unjust death on the cross in order to save her. Weep, then, for your Saviour, Héloïse, not for your betrayer. Weep for

your Redeemer, not for your seducer. If you persist in de-
ploring what you call my ruin, one might wonder if your
love is as pure as it is supposed to be. As Pompey said to
Cornelia: "Pompey has survived his battles, only his fortune is dead; when you weep now, it is for what you used
to love."[37]

Nothing can substitute for the actual reading of these
remarkable pages. They are as compressed as living tissues.
It is impossible to analyze them without sacrificing most of
their beauty. But the finest of all appear only at the end
when Abélard discusses the sufferings of which Héloïse
complains. He urges her to accept them for what they
really are: not as evils making a continual mockery of her
most exemplary monastic life, but as purifying tests win-
ning for her the martyr's crown. Let her accept her sufferings both for herself and for him. For if it is only too true
that he can no longer merit anything, Héloïse can henceforth suffer and expiate for both. Jesus Christ belongs to
Héloïse since she has become His spouse. But Abélard also
belongs to Héloïse, since they have been made one by marriage. Whatever belongs to Héloïse belongs equally to
Abélard, even Jesus Christ. "We are one in Christ. We
are one flesh by the law of marriage. Whatever you have,
I regard as mine. Now Christ is yours because you have
become His spouse. . . . It is in your strength at His side
that I place my hope, so as to obtain through your prayer
what I cannot obtain through my own." What more total,
more intimate union, what union higher and more worthy
of Héloïse's great soul could Abélard have offered her? He
is her servant. She is his master. He is giving her his soul
to be ransomed by her sufferings. He is powerless to save

it himself because he is no longer capable of suffering. Hé-loïse ought to know that she is the real victor because she at least can suffer and can struggle on. She alone, therefore, can be victorious: "He who is still in the field can still carry the day. I can no longer return a conqueror because I have no more battles to fight." Thus it is that Abélard insists on calling Héloïse his lord—*Dominus*—because it is only she who is fighting, only she who can win for both of them the one remaining battle of salvation.

The moving prayer which Abélard begs the Abbess to say for them and with which he brings his letter to an end, reveals Abélard at his best:

"O God, who from the beginning of the creation of mankind, hast, in fashioning the woman from a rib of the man, consecrated the very great mystery of the nuptial union; Thou who hast highly honored marriage by being Thyself born in wedlock and by performing Thy first miracle at the wedding feast of Cana; Thou who hast in the past granted, in such manner as it has pleased Thee to do it, this remedy to my incontinence and weakness, scorn not the prayers which I, Thy humble servant, suppliantly place before the face of Thy Majesty for my own disorders and for those of him whom I love. Pardon, O very merciful God, rather, O Thou who art mercy itself, pardon even sins as great as ours, and let the immensity of Thy unspeakable mercy be measured by the multitude of our faults. Punish now, I beg of Thee, the guilty ones so that they may be spared in the future. Punish them in time to spare them in eternity. Lift against Thy servants the rod of correction, not the sword of wrath. Punish their flesh to save their souls. Come as a Redeemer not as an Avenger, as a God of clemency rather than of justice, as a merciful Father not as a stern Lord. Test us, O Lord, and try us, but rather as the Prophet would have you deal with him: 'Test me, O Lord, and try me, burn in the crucible my loins and my heart' (Psalm 25:2), that is to say: examine first my strength, and measure out accordingly the burden of my temptations. This is what St. Paul promised the faithful when he said: 'God will not play you false; he will not allow you to be tempted beyond your powers. With the temptation itself, he will ordain the issue of it, and enable you to hold your own' (I Cor. 10:13). It is Thou, O Lord, who hast brought us together, and Thou hast parted us when and as it pleased Thee. The work which Thou didst begin in mercy, finish today in a multitude of mercies, and those whom Thou hast parted for a time in this world, unite forever in the next, O Thou, our hope, our inheritance, our expectation, our consolation, Lord who art blest forever. Amen."[38]

The penitent who was one day to make his peace with St. Bernard and to die in total renunciation, is already totally present in these lines. Abélard knew how to climb this summit. We may fear that he strove in vain to lift Héloïse to the same height. We should like to be able to say that she was won by this eloquence and accepted this high ideal of Christian charity, and that she came finally to love Abélard for God, rather than God for Abélard, or even, as was the case, Abélard against God. If she ever submitted, it was in the hidden recesses of her heart, not openly in her letters.

Her submission, accordingly, is not a part of recorded history. As far as we are concerned, the bitter debate which brought these two great souls into conflict, ends with Abélard's Christian submission to Providence in the joy of sacrifice, and with Héloïse's acceptance of the Stoic principles which she found in Seneca and Lucan.

VI

The Mystery of Héloïse

IT IS not too difficult to extract from our texts a picture of Héloïse that is at one and the same time simple and clear. But the Héloïse thus discovered, though possibly historically real and certainly consistent with documentary evidence, is most improbable. The evidence points to a Héloïse who is all lover, who is an incarnation of the pure essence of love to the exclusion of everything else. We can add, however, that if she is the great lover, she is so in the French manner, with that strange yearning for rational or sophistical justification to be encountered in Chrétien de Troyes, in Corneille, and even, alas, in Rousseau. If this demands further testimony, we have the word of Henry Adams, whose perspicacity borders on genius: "The twelfth century, with all its sparkle, would be dull without Abélard and Héloïse. With infinite regret, Héloïse must be left out of the story, because she was not a philosopher or a poet or an artist, but only a Frenchwoman to the last millimeter of her shadow. Even though one may suspect that her famous letters to Abélard are, for the most part, by no means above scepticism, she was, by French standards, worth at least a dozen Abélards, if only because she called St. Bernard a false apostle. Unfortunately, French standards, by which she must be judged in our ignorance, take for granted that she philosophized only for the sake of Abélard, while Abélard taught philosophy to her not so much because he believed in philosophy or in her as because he believed in himself. To this day, Abélard remains a problem as perplexing as he must have been to Héloïse, and almost as fascinating. As the west portal of Chartres is the door through which one must of necessity enter the Gothic architecture of the thirteenth century, so Abélard is the portal of approach to the Gothic thought and philosophy within. Neither art nor thought has a modern equivalent; only Héloïse, like Isolde, unites the ages."[1]

That a woman should rival a myth in sheer realism is, indeed, a remarkable occurrence! Proof is not wanting that Héloïse was much like this, and no one will insist upon more. Nevertheless, what remains to be noticed is essentially different from what we have seen hitherto. For it will not hereafter be a question of a learned young woman seduced by the famous master, but of something far more significant, the Abbess of the Paraclete. When we read her letters, we hear the voice of a woman, still young, to be sure, yet one to whom has been entrusted the important spiritual offices of prioress and abbess in two Benedictine houses. But reading her letters, one is struck immediately by the omnipresence of Abélard and the total absence of God. Nor can this fact be passed off by merely saying that God is absent from the letters. He is continually being expelled from them. How are we to explain an attitude like this?

We know from Abélard himself that when he sought refuge in the monastic life, neither fervor nor religious vocation played a very large rôle in his decision. He was obeying neither God's call nor the command of Héloïse. He wanted to hide his shame; and this was about all. Héloïse's entry into religion, if externally like Abélard's, was basically very different. No more, of course, than he, was she answering an interior call. She was acting out of deference to Abélard's orders. When formerly she had offered to be his mistress and he had preferred that she become his wife, she had done as he wished. Now, when he wanted her to become a religious, she became this too, simply because it was a further mark of the love he expected of her and which she was powerless to refuse. Again, her sacrifice was immediate and without reservation either in thought or act. Her action here was the more meritorious in that Abélard, if he had not actually misjudged it, had at least found means to render it odious. For he was not satisfied that she should merely enter religion, but he insisted that she enter before he did. He was not, in his heart, even then sure of her! She did as he asked and submitted to the outrage, but she was never able to forget it.

On this important point, as indeed on all the others, the testimony of both Abélard and Héloïse is in complete accord. "She, however, spontaneously took the veil first, at my command" *(Illa tamen prius ad imperium nostrum sponte velata)*, says Abélard, indicating that before he himself entered Saint-Denys, Héloïse had promised to take the veil *at his command*. Several, he adds, tried vainly to frighten her, depicting the monastic rule as too heavy a yoke for youth to bear. But in vain. Their pity could not break her resolve. "Mingled with tears and sobs, the lament of Cornelia escaped as best it could from her lips: 'Illustrious spouse, for whom my bed was unworthy, what rights did destiny possess over your noble head? How great was my sin in marrying you, if I was to make you so miserable? Accept this day my expiation, for it is of my own accord that I offer it.' "² "Saying these words" *(in his verbis)* "she rushed towards the altar, accepted unflinchingly the veil blessed by the bishop, and consecrated herself publicly to the religious life."³ When this scene took place, Héloïse could hardly have been twenty years old.

Abélard's account is of capital importance because its every word is full of significance. Even the apparent contradiction in its first phrase is significant: *At the command* of Abélard, Héloïse *spontaneously* took the veil. When it was Abélard who commanded, immediate obedience was her only course. But her reasons for obeying Abélard's command were supremely personal. Héloïse knew only too well what lay behind Abélard's decision. When we examine his reasons, we see that they do him little honor. In demanding that Héloïse enter religion, Abélard was depriving her of the only consolation remaining to her—expiation for her crime of marrying him. Thus Héloïse accepts Abélard's order; but only for her own reasons will she do what he asks. The action to which he forces her will have no other significance than she chooses to give it. And this significance has no religious character whatsoever. The verses of Lucan's *Pharsalia* which she stammers out as she hastens towards the altar are too expressive for one to misunderstand the exact value she was assigning her act. There would be something naïve in believing that she could really have recited these verses, if it was not still more naïve to doubt it. They express her intentions so perfectly that one wonders if it was not the intentions which suggested the verses. The idea of renouncing the world, not for God, not even to expiate the offenses committed against God, but for Abélard and to expiate the crime which she had committed against Abélard, assuredly indicate in Héloïse a singular indifference to the Christian sense of the act which she is performing. But if the sentiment motivating her is not Christian, it is completely Roman and not at all unworthy of Cornelia from whose words she borrows. If we must believe what Abélard indicates, Héloïse regarded her religious profession only as an expiatory sacrifice to the hero whom she had destroyed by marrying him.

One is forced to believe this because what Abélard suggests so precisely and discreetly, Héloïse later affirms with all the force and insistence of which she was capable, when it was a question of removing all equivocation as to the "purity" of her sentiments. "Since at *your* command I changed at once both dress and mind to show you to be *sole* possessor of both my body and my soul . . ." (col. 184D). Since Abélard is the *sole* possessor of Héloïse's soul, God has then *no* part in this religious profession—"Not devotion to religion but your command alone drew me, young as I was, to embrace the severities of monastic life" (col. 186C). It is only Abélard's *command*, and *no* devotion whatsoever, which determined this taking of the veil. And as if these statements were still not sufficiently clear, Héloïse goes so far as to state precisely that God owes her no recompense for what she has done, because from the time of her entrance into religion she has done nothing out of love for Him: "Over and above this [that is, any favor Abélard might show her] I can expect no reward from

God, for I am sure that up to now I have done nothing out
of love for Him" (col. 186D). It is not then for God but
for Abélard that the Abbess of the Paraclete works; for just
as he alone can make her suffer, so *he alone* can console
her: "For you alone can make me sad, you alone can make
me happy or bring me consolation." (col. 184C). How
could Abélard have doubted for an instant one who, at a
word from him, had preceded him when he was going to
God? This cruel want of confidence filled her with such
sorrow and shame, that the very memory of the affront is
enough to send Héloïse into a raging passion. To follow
him into the convent or to precede him there, what difference to her? "God knows, I would not have hesitated to
follow you or to precede you into hell itself *(ad Vulcania
loca)* if you had given the order. My heart was not my
own, but yours. Even now, more than ever before, if it is
not with you it is nowhere, for you are its very existence.
So, I pray you, let my poor heart be happy with you. And
it will be happy with you if it finds you gentle, if you render
it grace for grace, little things for great, words for things.
Remember, I beg you, everything I have done; and weigh
out all that you owe me. When I delighted with you in
carnal pleasures *(libido)*, many wondered why I did it,
whether it was for concupiscence or for love. But now my
last state shows my true beginning, and I now forgo all
pleasures only to obey your will. Truly, I reserved nothing for myself but to be yours before everything, and such
I am to this very moment."[4]

Such words are too clear for any mistaking of the true
nature of Héloïse's feelings. The seventeenth century will
know women ready to endure hell for the love of God, but

the love of Abélard is quite enough to make Héloïse willing to seek the realm of Vulcan. He speaks, his servant listens. Of old, at a word from him, she gave herself up to the most violent carnal pleasures. Now, at another word from him, she condemns herself to the severest rigors of the monastic life. She not only thinks of it this way, but writes to him to this effect, for she wishes him to know it. He must know it, indeed, lest he come to think that Héloïse had found in the cloister the calm, the peace, and the consolations of divine love. No doubt, it was that she might find these things that Abélard gave her up. But he simply must know that it is not for God but for him that she is in the cloister. What does it really matter where she is? She would go to hell itself at his bidding. Only Abélard must know that she has become a religious for the same reason that she had become his mistress. What others call giving themselves to God was for her but another way of giving herself to him.

It has been necessary to examine all these minute details to understand the terrible anguish that lies behind Héloïse's first letter. It is literally the distress of a worshipper forsaken by her god. The comparison is not too strong, for although Héloïse never dared write it, she never ceases to suggest it. The least love of God, so it seems to her, would be a theft from the exclusive love vowed forever to Abélard and reserved exclusively for him. In consternation at these sentiments, Abélard undertakes the impossible in trying to make her renounce them. His efforts were put forth in vain. Neither God nor Abélard could ever make Héloïse deny the reality of her passion. Save to reproach him, Héloïse speaks of God only to call Him to witness that she does not think first of Him, do anything first for Him, nor hope for anything first from Him. "Whatever the state of my life, God knows I still fear more to offend you than to offend Him. It is you rather than He that I desire to please. It is not out of love of God, but at your request that I entered religion."[5] Abélard got Héloïse to do everything, save to pretend to love God a little more than him.

It has been necessary to push things thus far in order to discover the full sense of certain expressions which Héloïse employs in speaking of her taking of the veil. Even Abélard, in the few gripping lines he devotes to this scene, carefully notes the tragic outburst with which Héloïse undertook her sacrifice. "Thereupon she rushed to the altar and quickly took the veil" *(Mox properat, confestim velum tulit)*. Clearly, she threw herself passionately into the cloister. At no moment in her life, indeed, did she give herself quite so passionately to Abélard. Of old, at a word from him, she agreed to lose herself for his sake. But this was still just a matter of love because Abélard was only asking for what she desired herself. Her entry into religion was quite another thing. It was no longer love, but madness, because in her very excess of love she separated herself forever from the one being she loved.[6] Here are no conventional formulas, but the plainest conceivable expression of the most genuine feelings and the most incontestable facts. If Héloïse's taking of the veil was not her tenderest and most passionate sacrifice for the love of Abélard, one wonders what more she could possibly have given him.

It is true, of course, that Abélard was giving a command. But by no divine law was it her duty to obey. Abélard's mutilation, his decision to hide his shame in a cloister were

certainly not for Héloïse the equivalent of a religious vocation. Fifteen years later, as Abbess of the Paraclete, she still
felt the want of this. All she really wanted—*quod solum
appetebat*—as we already know, was what she was actually
giving up, Abélard himself. In his ruin, she loves him more
than ever, and never for an instant dreams of being separated from him. What matter the pleasures lost? She has
told us clearly enough that it was not the pleasures but himself she loved. It is enough for her that he still lives, provided
that a long life of happiness by his side is still possible. This
happiness he could not take from her save by her own consent. If Héloïse were to refuse to enter religion, Abélard
himself could not enter either. He was her husband, she his
wife, and even leaving out of consideration their child (who
never seems to be considered in this affair), it was only the
mutual consent of the spouses that could separate them. We
can well imagine what spirit of sacrifice it required for her
to become a religious before Abélard and to forego all that
was left to her of a love to which she had already sacrificed
everything.

When we follow Héloïse to this point, to the very core
of her conscience, remarks which might otherwise have
struck us as cynical and even blasphemous, are redeemed by
a basic truthfulness and simple honesty. To say that they
are only human is not to make them less true or less honest.
We see here, more than anywhere else, how much better
it is to read the story in its basic texts than simply to imagine
it. When all is said, what has Héloïse actually told us?
That she entered religion without a religious vocation?
Certainly. That at the moment of writing the letters, this
vocation had not yet come? She seems to think so, in any

case, and it may well be true.[7] That as Abbess of the Paraclete, she had never found the strength to love God above
all things else, because Abélard was still her first love? Perhaps she was far closer to divine charity than many others
who dethrone God for a great deal less than Abélard, or
who do not even so much as recall what is the greatest and
the first commandment.

Historians, treating of Héloïse, ought never to forget a
cautionary remark of St. Teresa of Avila, which might well
have had her in mind: "I am surprised at your saying you
know this young woman merely from having seen her. We
women are not easy to know. Even when you have been
their confessor for many years, you are surprised yourself
to have understood them so badly. They do not, in expos-
ing their faults, give an exact account of themselves; and
you are wrong to judge them only from what they tell
you." What exactly was the spiritual life of Héloïse? Since
she perhaps never knew this herself, I willingly admit that
we will never know either. Still it is true to say that Heloïse's confidences are not those of a religious who has failed
in her vocation or who is in revolt against the divine sum-
mons, but rather the plaints of a simple woman forced by
the despotic will of her lover to tackle an insoluble problem.
Her problem is to find in the passion this man inspires the
strength required for a life of sacrifice which is both mean-
ingless and impossible save on the level of the love of God.
Such is the crisis through which the Abbess of the Paraclete
is struggling. Nothing could be more poignant than this
spiritual misery. The whole thing is so cruelly clear to her
that she prefers to put up with it rather than lie about it,
even if lying about it could help her to forget it.

The despairing call of Héloïse to Abélard is therefore a great deal more than the protest of a forsaken lover. It is a cry for help to the man whose call she had answered when she entered religion. Even had she wished it at the time, she would not have been able to answer a divine call which could not be heard. There was no question of her making such a sacrifice for God. God had not asked it. Since she had never done anything to deserve a call to perfection, she thought she had no reason to expect one. But Abélard had demanded all of her. He had even asked her to accept this burden which was so heavy that she felt she had not grace to bear it. Was he not then bound to help her, bound to direct her, bound to sustain her with his knowledge and strength? Was it not his strict duty to help her to bear a burden which he, and not God, had determined she should bear?

To reread Héloïse's letters on this point is to understand the exact nature of the absence of God which they reveal. It is also to see from their bright perspective so many specific details impossible to observe from any other. If God is not there, it is not because she has refused Him, but because He has refused Himself to her. At least, Héloïse thinks this. So it is that with a total religious humility, of which she alone seems not to know the cost, she undertakes the most trying austerities without so much as thinking that God will ever reckon them to her credit.[8] Perhaps it is not by chance that she associates her acceptance of the cloister with an acceptance of hell itself, because the monastic life which she unflinchingly lives without divine consolations is in her eyes nothing short of a state of penal expiation. But now—redoubled misery proceeding from the same cause—she feels that she is beyond the state in which she can merit anything and, by the same token, in which she can expiate for anything. Héloïse only took the veil for Abélard. Since it is only the intention that counts, not one of all her sacrifices is an act of expiation in the eyes of God. They are, all of them, sacrifices for Abélard.

Her obstinate reproaching of God has no other cause. It is only intelligible as an expression of spiritual misery. In fact, one can say that from the beginning to the end of their common life, Abélard led Héloïse from one impossible situation to another—from fornication to a secret marriage, from a secret marriage to religious profession without a vocation, from religious profession to the responsibilities of an abbess and to a penitential life for which she was capable of sacrifice but not of true penitence. As for expiating for a marriage which caused the mutilation of Abélard, that she could do: "For this offense above all, I hope I can do fitting penance". Héloïse does not shirk a long life of penance and contrition for this act: "that at the very least by a long life of sorrow and penance, I may somehow do my share to compensate for your punishment and suffering." She unreservedly accepts this punishment of her crime. And we should be quite wrong if we thought she ever even considered rebelling against the monastic state in which she lived. It was not too penitential a life to expiate those hours of pain through which Abélard had passed:[9] "That what you have suffered in the body for a passing hour, I may suffer in anguish of soul throughout my life, as I deserve, and so make satisfaction to you at least, if not to God."[10] The subject of this complaint is penance done for Abélard's sake, not for God.

Héloïse is always precise and positive. Thus she points out the two principal reasons which prevent her severest mortifications from being acts of true penance. First, she never actually accepted the cruel blow which God had struck them. This was her "old and stubborn complaint" which Abélard found so tiresome. Héloïse never admitted that God, having spared them when they were living in fornication, should have punished them so cruelly after they were married. The Sacrament had redressed the evils of their disorderly life. Then, because of the marriage, they are visited with the kind of punishment which might better have been meted out for adultery. Thus, she says to Abélard, you are punished for a marriage which was actually repairing the injury done to all the parties concerned. The misfortune which adulterous women bring down upon their lovers, your own wife occasioned for you. What is more, we were not even sharing the joys of marriage when you were thus punished. For the moment we were separated. You were living chastely in Paris, directing the schools; I was at Argenteuil where, at your bidding, I was living with the religious. Thus when we were separated from each other, you to devote more zeal to your schools, I to have more time for prayer and meditation on the Holy Scriptures, when our life was becoming more holy and more chaste, you suffered in your body for a sin which the two of us had committed together. In brief, in humbling himself to the extent of marrying her, Abélard had so fully expiated for all his sins that the very justice of God ought to have spared him.[11] But God did not wish to spare him, and it is this that Héloïse cannot bring herself to forgive. Henceforth how could she do penance for having drawn on Abélard a divine punishment which she herself declares unjust? It is not she but the supreme cruelty of God that is responsible.[12] Héloïse knows that as long as she feels this way about it, she is offending God and rebelling against Providence. She cannot expiate before God the ruin she has brought upon Abélard so long as she does not recognize the justice of the blow which she and Abélard have been dealt.

Nor is this all. How can Héloïse do penance even for the guilty pleasures of the past while she is still in her heart longing for them? To confess her faults is easy. It is equally easy to mortify her body and to inflict exterior penances. But it is very hard to uproot from her heart the desire for supreme carnal pleasures.[13] And such had been those of these lovers—so sweet, says Héloïse, that she cannot hate them nor without great effort drive them from her memory: "When I ought to be lamenting over what I have done, I am rather sighing for what I have lost."[14] Far from moaning over what she has done, she sighs after what she has lost. Who will deliver Héloïse from this body of death? How much more mercifully has not God dealt with Abélard? Like a good physician, He has not hesitated to make him suffer in order to save him. God was never kinder to him than when He seemed to treat him like a pitiless enemy. But Héloïse is young. The burning ardor of the desires of youth and the experience of sweetest pleasures overwhelm a heart too feeble to resist them. Her friends extol her chastity, the rigor of her austerities, the exemplary dignity of her religious life. But it is a question here of acts, which count for nothing, not of intention which counts for everything. "They say I am chaste, because they have not discovered that I am a hypocrite."[15] Men see what she does. They cannot see what she thinks. But God sees all, He who is the searcher of loins and of hearts. It is something perhaps not to commit evil, and, by forced intention, to avoid scandal in the Church. No doubt even some grace is necessary for this. But to avoid evil is not enough, it is necessary also to do good. Only that is good which is done for the love of God. Héloïse does nothing, save for the love of Abélard. It is to please him that she has accepted this way of life. It is for him that she is putting up with it. Everyone, and Abélard most of all, is being taken in by it. Everyone, God excepted, mistakes this hypocrisy for religion: "My dissimulation long deceived you as it did many others, so that you mistook my hypocrisy for religion" (*diu te, sicut multos, simulatio mea fefellit, ut religioni deputares hypocrisin*). Thus, this miserable life of hers, which counts for nothing with God because it is not for Him she lives it, she must live alone, because even Abélard is deceived to the point that he is abandoning her to herself, and, rather than pray for her, is asking Héloïse to pray for him.[16]

In a phrase, the hidden meaning of this passionate complaint is that the absence of God makes the absence of Abélard seem far more cruel and unpardonable. It is not unjust that God, for whom she does nothing, should desert her. But it is most unjust that Abélard, for whom she does everything, should forsake her. Such are the last personal reflections which Héloïse has confided to us. Nothing, not a single line, justifies our thinking that she ever changed. Urged by Abélard to adopt an attitude towards God more in conformity with her state, she prefers to change the topic; for as long as Abélard was there, it would be quite

impossible for her not to start in all over again. Thus
Héloïse is reduced to silence, but for the same motives that
ruled all her other acts—obedience: "Lest perchance you
be able to allege that I have been wanting somewhat in
obedience."[17] After this, we shall have still another letter
from her, one marked by steadiness and good sense dealing
with the conditions which must be satisfied by a religious
rule for women. This is followed by forty-two questions,
all rather dry, on various passages of Holy Scripture. Then,
silence. We never know whether this was a disciplinary
silence, once more carrying out the will of Abélard, or
whether it was a kind of reconciliation to the will of God.
We shall never know, and there are few reasons, humanly
speaking, to suspect the latter. The iron will she everywhere displayed would hardly allow her to betray the passion in which she gloried. She could refuse to speak about
it. But nothing from her pen has ever denied it.

When all is said and done, the true Héloïse is simple
enough. The complicated analysis of her feelings with
which we have been concerned here depends less on what
she was in herself than on the predicament in which she
found herself. These complications are well expressed in
the superscription to her first letter: "To her lord, or rather,
father; to her husband, or rather, brother; from his servant,
or rather daughter; his wife, or rather, sister: to Abélard
from Héloïse."[18] And later: "To her only one after Christ,
she who is his only one in Christ."[19] Lastly, and above all,
the astonishing and untranslatable abridgement in the last
letter: *Domino specialiter, sua singulariter;*[20] that is, "to God
in special, to him in particular." For in so far as concerns
the logical species—the nun—she is the Lord's, but as an

individual she is Abélard's. After a superscription like this, the sense of which was perfectly clear to her professor of logic, she can go on to write about other things, keeping her resolve to speak no more of her inner feelings. He has just made a mighty effort to make Héloïse understand that she is now the spouse of Christ. She replies without a direct word on the matter, but merely in the heading of her letter: Yes, I belong to the species of the spouses of Christ, but there is only one woman who is Abélard's wife, and I am that too. Héloïse is Abélard's wife. She has been recruited into the religious life, a state of perfection for which she neither has the vocation nor feels the grace. She has but one natural support to sustain herself in her role—the love she bears her husband.

There is nothing inconceivable in all this, nor anything further admissible if we adhere to the texts that come down to us. And if it is to this conclusion that history brings us, history will never take us any further. Perhaps history is proposing a problem here that is itself insoluble. No one has put it better than Charles de Rémusat, when he wrote: "Héloïse submitted to the will of Abélard, and for his sake to all the obligations of her state. Out of deference to the religious in her, she hid the devotion of the wife. . . . But inconsolable and undaunted, she obeyed and did not give in. She accepted all her obligations without much ado about them; and her soul never loved its virtues."[21] There is not a word in this firmly stated judgment which does not express the truth which is to be found in the documents. And yet, although he appears not to notice it, what a fearful problem de Rémusat raises when he formulates this judgment! For if these words mean anything at all, they mean

that Héloïse lived an irreproachable religious life for forty
years without having received the graces for it, and forty
years of the severest penance without any faith in its religious efficacy.[22] Abélard refused to believe that these were
Héloïse's sentiments, though, as we can see, he was in a
position to do so. The responsibility for so terrible a tragedy
was far too heavy for him not to have hesitated to deny its
existence. He accused her, therefore, merely of coquetry.
The human heart is complex and its most sincerely tragic
sentiment can be accompanied by others that are less tragic.
For Héloïse to have wished to tell the whole world about
her sorrow was still a little less noble than to endure it in
silence. That she may have found a sort of bitter pleasure
in this is not impossible. That she may have taken pleasure
in her misfortune as her surest claim to glory and that this
pleasure may have been mingled with bitterness is almost
certain. But when all this is shown, it can in no way be concluded that the sentiments she reveled in were not really
her own nor that they were less profound than they were
sincere. No man can scrutinize consciences. Héloïse herself did not know everything about her own case. At least,
however, she never lied about it. But if she did not know
everything, it is ridiculous for us to pretend to know more.
Whether we find her case mysterious or not, we have to
accept it as it stands.

VII

The End of the Drama

THIS unforgettable dialogue has now come to an end and two great hearts have ceased therein to make each other suffer. From now on all vanishes into a void which our imagination vainly seeks to penetrate. The more closely we study the letters, the more we are convinced that such interlocutors are irreplaceable. If either of them has invented the letters of the other, or if some unknown author has disguised his work under the names of the two famous lovers, we can be certain, without any fear of error, that this ingenious forger was one of the most powerful creative writers known to any literature. We could no more find his like than we could find another Héloïse and Abélard. There would be nothing further to say had not Peter the Venerable appeared on the scene at the conclusion of this story, like the messenger in some ancient drama come to recite the hero's end.

While Héloïse takes refuge in her duties as abbess, Abélard continues the tumultuous career which his fatal genius never ceases to fashion for him. He is one whose infallible instinct leads straight to dangerous questions and provoking replies. He is an adventurer of the mind, a discoverer of new lands who plots his course where his pioneer's instinct leads him. Bernard of Clairvaux follows him, watches him, and becomes uneasy. He too, severe guardian of orthodoxy that he is, has a taste for adventure, but seeks it, not in the realm of reason, but in that of love. How sharply the two of them disagree! Abélard forges ahead, swept onward by the brilliance of his intellect which is so open and so imprudently generous. Bernard is afraid of this continual agitation which seems to him so unregulated. It is something foreign to his nature, something he mistrusts and which he is apt to see everywhere, even where it is not. No eloquence, no dialectic can prevail against the hard uncompromising nature of the saint in a struggle for something in his eyes most sacred. The rash doctrines of Abélard were finally condemned by the Council of Sens. After 1141, the man whom his adversary called Goliath was no more than a beaten giant, wounded to death but struggling violently to raise himself.

During these cruel hours, overwhelmed by the condemnation of his doctrine, the Christian philosopher doubts whether he should follow his truth or his God. But Abélard resolutely chooses Christ. Who can tell the effect on his decision of the silent presence of the stern yet tender abbess who was following the Council from afar in an anguish of heart easy to divine? Once more, she was in the center of the drama: Ought the abbess who had no vocation add to so many sacrifices the tardy revelation that she had given herself to God for the love of a man himself rejected by God? In a last letter, to which there is no answer and which seems not to have demanded one, Abélard recites for her the profession of faith which Bernard of Clairvaux was unable to wring from him. Here, for those who can read it, is the greatest testimony Héloïse ever received of his love and respect.

"Héloïse, my sister, once so dear in the world, today still more dear in Jesus Christ, logic has won for me the hatred of men. Perverse perverters, for whom Wisdom is a kind of hell, are saying that I am a great logician but that I am considerably mistaken in my interpretation of St. Paul. They acknowledge the keenness of my mind but doubt the purity of my Christian faith. Here, at least so it seems to me, they are like men frightened by opinion rather than instructed by experience.

"I do not wish to be a philosopher if this means that I must reject St. Paul. I do not wish to be an Aristotle if this means that I must separate myself from Christ, for 'this alone of all the names under heaven has been appointed to men as the one by which we must needs be saved' (Acts 4:12). I adore Christ, who reigns at the right hand of the Father. I clasp Him with the arms of faith, when by the divine power He performs glorious works in a virginal flesh born from the Paraclete. And to banish all restless solicitude, all doubt from the heart that beats in your breast, I want you to have this from my pen: I have established my conscience on that rock on which Christ built his Church. Here, briefly, is the inscription it bears.

"I believe in the Father, the Son, and the Holy Ghost, God in one nature, the true God in whom the Trinity of Persons in no way affects the unity of substance. I believe that the Son is the equal of the Father in all things, in eternity, in power, in will, in operation. I do not hold with Arius who with a perverse spirit, or rather seduced by a diabolical spirit, introduces grades into the Trinity, maintaining that the Father is greater, the Son less great, as though forgetting the precept of faith: 'Thou shalt not mount by degrees to my altar' (Exod. 20:26). For to place a before and after in the Trinity is to mount the altar of God by degrees. I attest that the Holy Ghost is equal and consubstantial in all things with the Father and the Son, for it is He whom I often call in my books by the name of Goodness. I condemn Sabellius who held that the Person of the Father is the same as that of the Son, and believed that the Father suffered the Passion, whence the name Patripassians. I believe also that the Son of God became the Son of Man in such a way that the one only person *consists* and subsists in two natures; that the same Son of God satisfied all the exigencies of the human condition which He assumed, even death itself, and that He revived and ascended into Heaven whence He shall come to judge the living and the dead. I affirm, finally, that all sins are remitted by baptism; that we need grace to begin good and to accomplish it, and that those who have fallen are restored by penance. Need I speak of the resurrection of the flesh? I shall call myself a Christian in vain if I did not believe that I should one day live again.

"This is the faith in which I live and from which my hope derives its strength. In this refuge I do not fear the noise of Scylla; I laugh at the whirlpool of Charybdis; nor do I fear the mortal chant of the Sirens. Let the tempest come; it will not shake me! The winds may blow, but I shall not be moved. The rock of my foundation is sure."

All that should be said is here said. Nor will Abélard, any more than Héloïse, brook contradiction even once. In this final testament, written for her who was "dear to him

in this world", he does not deny their love. He seeks her
out to witness his faith, and he entrusts his written testimony to her hands, assured that she can both receive and
guard it. Abélard's security is his faith; and his faith is
secure in the hands of Héloïse. He entrusts her with his
unreserved adhesion to the faith of the Fathers—the only
faith he recognized. He might have spoken imprudently
about it at times, but he never wittingly betrayed it. Here
he is, then, reciting his creed. It is the creed of all Christians.
But being Abélard, he cannot recite it in the usual manner.
The Paraclete and the Good still haunt his memory; and
the impenitent humanist is unwilling to conclude this solemn profession of faith, written during the hours of trial,
without mobilizing once more the Sirens of the Aeneid.
After all, he can be asked to retract but he cannot be asked
to change.

Secure in his conscience, Abélard is not yet convinced
that he is wrong. His persecutors have not yet got him to
admit the errors they reproach him with. The tired old
warrior feels that he has not yet spoken his final word.
He appeals to Rome. When Innocent II also condemns him
for heresy and asks him henceforth to remain silent and to
deliver his writings to the fire, he sets out himself for the
Eternal City, still hoping to gain a hearing and perhaps even
to justify himself.

The moment our questions become precise, history refuses to give an answer. We should like to know the first
stages of the journey now undertaken by Abélard. But
save that he set out, a man old at sixty years, battered and
worn by so many encounters, we know almost nothing.
The route from Paris to Rome was long for one who had

to walk it and hard for a poor man wanting the normal means of livelihood. He passed, we are told, from monastery to monastery. Probably this is true. But what kind of reception could he receive as he moved along? The sentence of the Council was upon his head, condemning him to silence, and, if it was literally carried out, even to sequestration. Since his former state was so high, his fall was a great one and we can only experience a kind of pity as we see him move from one door to the next, finding, no doubt, some that were slow to open to take him in. Letters of Bernard of Clairvaux were preceding him to Rome, and who can be sure that their contents had been kept secret? Peter's enemy had no need to seek shelter with Peter's successor. Even the shelter which every Christian expects as he approached the Holy Father was being closed to him in advance. How we should have enjoyed gazing upon his countenance, making our mental journey along the way with him, lightening that cross which can have been no less heavy because carried in the heart.

But we shall know nothing of all this, save that one day he arrived at Cluny, near Mâcon, a city rather than a monastery, mother of so many abbeys, renowned throughout Europe for the splendor of her church, the beauty of her worship, and the warmness of her hospitality. Peter the Venerable was abbot at the time, as Abélard knew; and we can well surmise that as he raised his hand to knock on the door he was confident that it would open for him.

It is painful to explain this confidence, even when it is proven to have been justified. But Cluny had its reasons for receiving kindly the vanquished victim of Citeaux. They knew all about St. Bernard, ever since the fiery Abbot of

Clairvaux had launched his terrifying attack against them. The two abbeys had had their difficulties to iron out. On these occasions, Bernard had used language about Peter likely to incline Cluny to accept at considerably less than its face value anything he had to say about Abélard. Above all, his celebrated *Apology* for Cistercian life which so harshly criticized the "superfluities" of Cluny was likely to soften the hearts of those from whom Abélard was asking for hospitality. Nor must they have taken too literally all the condemnations hurled by the saint. Let us go further. Without attempting to establish the least connection between Cluny and some of those speculations to which it was always a stranger, we must recognize that there was a hidden relationship, though on a different level, between what Bernard disliked in Abélard and what he condemned at Cluny. It was the "world" and its corrupting influence on the religious life. To accuse the Clunyites of "intemperance" in eating and drinking, clothing and furniture, taste for horses and love of fine buildings, is no slight reproach, above all if we take into account the often crude language in which it was put. Bernard even condemned the beauty of their churches and their art for what J. K. Huysmans later calls with approval "luxury for God".

This little monastic quarrel was not serious, but it had doubtless left its marks. Nor had many years passed since 1138 when Bernard, addressing himself to the Pope, had accused his "Cluny friends" of "fraud and rashness". We can take these things in the spirit of charity, but they are unpleasant. Abbot Peter had replied in the same tone, asking "this new race of Pharisees" by what right they, who were living like the others, regarded themselves as "the only

true monks in the whole world".[1] But let us forget this
bickering. Peter the Venerable was not a man lightly given
to secret collusion. To receive Abélard into his house in
the spirit of perfect charity, he had only to be himself.
Peter may well have recalled, in view of his not so distant
experience, that the holy violence of Bernard sometimes
went beyond moderation. But he certainly knew, first and
foremost, that the tired, poor, condemned, and sorrowing
pilgrim who came seeking refuge was a guest sent by Christ
Himself.

This was the spirit in which he took him in. But we can
only marvel at the inexhaustibly inventive genius of Peter's
unequaled and upright generosity. There is no other word
to describe it; Peter the Venerable is perfect. We are here
privileged to assist at a spectacle, rare because an absolute
masterpiece, in which Christian love of neighbor does what
is expected of it and does it exactly in the way it should,
does it without fear and with no want of tact, risks everything at one stroke, and succeeds completely. First he has
to detain Abélard. The tired old man was not going to
reach Rome anyway. And since his purpose for going there
was to seek the peace of Christ, why might he not find it
right here in Cluny? The abbot begins to move. Since the
man he is dealing with is important, he quickly informs Pope
Innocent II of all the steps. I hesitate to tamper with this
letter by so irreplaceable a witness. And if it is only a question of reading between the lines, why should I arrogate
the privilege to myself. Let the reader judge!

"Master Pierre, well-known, I believe, to Your Holiness,
passed by Cluny recently, on his way from France. We
asked him where he was going. He replied that he was tired

of the provocations of people who would accuse him of heresy, a thing he abhorred, and that he had appealed to the Apostolic See, seeking protection. We praised his intentions and urged him to hasten to that common refuge known to us all. Apostolic justice is, we told him, never-failing. It is denied to no one, be he stranger or pilgrim. We even promised him that he would find mercy with You, if he needed it.

"In the midst of all this, His Grace, the Abbot of Citeaux arrived and spoke with him and myself about some means of putting an end to his dispute with the Abbot of Clairvaux, which, indeed, was the real reason for his appeal to you. We, too, did our best to make peace between them, and we urged him to go with the Abbot of Citeaux to visit him. We further counseled him, if he had used language offensive to Christian ears, to consent, through the Abbot of Citeaux or some other wise and worthy persons, to curb his language henceforth and to remove it from his writings.

"This he did. He went there; and, on his return, told us that, thanks to the Abbot of Citeaux, he had renounced his past remarks and made his peace with the Abbot of Clairvaux. Meanwhile, under our advice, or rather, we believe, by divine inspiration, he decided to give up the tumult of the schools and of studies and to reside permanently in your Cluny. This decision seemed to us to be the proper one in view of his age, his weakness and his religious profession. Knowing, moreover, that his learning, which is not unknown to you, would be of great profit to the large family of our brethren, we acceded to his request. On the condition that it is agreeable to Your Holiness, we have, accordingly, gladly and earnestly authorized him to return with us, who, as you well know, are devotedly yours.

I, your devoted servant, whatever else I may be, therefore beg this favor of you; this convent of Cluny, so devoted to you, begs it; Pierre himself begs it, on his own
part, through us, and by the bearers of these presents who
are your sons, by this letter which he has asked us to write
you. Deign to direct that he spend the last days of his life
and of his old age, not perhaps so very many, in your house
of Cluny. Direct, too, that nothing be done to terminate
his stay in this abode where the wandering sparrow is so
pleased to have found a nest. For the sake of that honor
which you lavish on all good men, and for the love which
you have yourself towards him, grant that the shield of
your apostolic protection may cover him."[2]

We must admire the diplomacy of the great abbot. He
explains that Abélard is right in going to Rome to seek
justice. He will find it there, and even find pardon too, if
need be. It is only providential chance that has brought the
Abbot of Citeaux to Cluny to reconcile Abélard and the
Abbot of Clairvaux. The old master has agreed to refrain
from doubtful statements. Further divine intervention has
made him decide to remain at Cluny and to forego the con-
tests of the schools. Thus the monastery of Peter the Venerable is assured of the services of the most celebrated master
in all Christendom. Peter is asking, in fact, that Abélard's
condemnation be allowed to stand with all its punitive
clauses, with the one exception, for him considerable, that
he be allowed to teach. Peter the Venerable sees many advantages in this management. Why should not the super-
natural build on the occasions provided by the natural?
Charity is served thereby, and the monastery loses nothing.

The abbot is thus assuring himself, as our contemporaries would put it, of "exclusive rights" over Master Pierre Abélard.

It is hard at first to conceive that this bird feathered for tempest has really become the simple sparrow Peter the Venerable speaks of. But it is true, none the less. Whereas hitherto his very presence was accompanied by the rumblings of war, at Cluny all is calm. Peace descends at last upon him. There is not a monk in the abbey who does not witness his sanctity, his humility, and his piety. Unless I am mistaken, writes Peter the Venerable later on, I do not remember his equal in true humility. From all we can see, St. Germain was not more humble, nor St. Martin more completely divested of earthly riches. In this large monastery, where he was continually being shoved into places of honor, he appeared so poorly garbed that one might have taken him for the least of all.

It is pleasant, indeed, to find the Abbot of Cluny true to his best self right to the end of this history, and treating the victim of Sens not as he might someone stricken by the plague but like a guest of honor in a distinguished house. With what delicacy he gives these details to Héloïse after the death of Abélard! Peter knew her well. And if anything could alleviate her sorrow, it was the assurance which he alone was in a position to give, that her hero had ended his days among friends conscious of his greatness and willing to let him see it.

Abélard, however, lived only for penance. As he had once given in to pride, he now plunged into an excess of humility. As the Father Abbot walks in the place which the liturgy assigns him, at the end of the procession, he raises his eyes and looks at Abélard and is amazed that so celebrated a man can live so humbly. Any garment, any food, any drink is good enough for him. He wants only what is necessary and disapproves of superfluity both for himself and for others. Reading ceaselessly, often at prayer, he keeps rigorous silence save for the occasional familiar chat with his brethren or for some public discussion of theology into which he has been pressed. He offers the Holy Sacrifice as frequently as he is permitted, and almost every day after the abbot has restored him to favor with the Holy See. Does he actually teach? There is no real proof that within the framework of this conventual life, he regularly teaches. But Peter says that he was ever busy with the things of the mind: "His thinking, his speaking, his work turned continually towards theology, philosophy, and learning which he never ceased to meditate, to teach and to profess."

We must be content with the limited information of our texts. Why burden them with commentary? They would then tell no other story than that of our imagination. Peter the Venerable is a direct and eminent witness. He is the only one we have, and it is doubtful that Héloïse herself possessed any other. The months pass by, and Abélard's end approaches. "Simple and straightforward, fearing God and refraining from evil, consecrating to God the last days of his life", he forms a part of the life of Cluny. But he is physically exhausted. Touched by humiliating infirmities from which he suffers more than is usual, he clearly needs calm and repose, almost impossible in this large monastery. The abbot, ever attentive to his welfare, chose a new residence for him, the Monastery of Saint-Marcel, near Châ-

lons, the most suitably placed of all the abbeys of Bour-
gogne, near the city, but on the other side of the Saône.
There Abélard continued his life of study. He stayed with
his books as much as his infirmities would allow; and it can
be said of him as has been said of Gregory, that there was
never a moment when he was not praying, reading, writing,
or dictating.

Death finally comes, but it does not catch him unpre-
pared. The furtive visitor (as the Gospel puts it) found
him busy about holy things, wakeful, vigilant, his lamp
filled with oil and his conscience at rest in the sanctity of
his life. He falls seriously ill of a rapidly increasing malady
and finds himself at the very portal of death. With all piety,
he makes a profession of his Catholic faith, confesses his
sins and receives the Sacrament, and thus forsakes this life
for eternity. This is the unanimous testimony of the monks
of the Convent of Saint-Marcel in which he died April 21,
1142, at the age of sixty-three. There he was first buried.
There, too, seven centuries later, Lamartine came to pay
homage to his memory and to dream in the shadow of the
huge linden tree where, legend will have it, Abélard used
to sit in revery with his face "turned in the direction of the
Paraclete".[3]

All these final episodes, after the Council of Sens, took
place within a period of two years during which Héloïse
seems not to have been in communication with Abélard.
"She lived in deep silence", writes de Rémusat; "and for
long years her great heart was shut, revealing itself to no
one but God, not even giving itself to Him. We know
nothing about her."[4] No, not even that her heart remained
closed to God! But we do know that Abélard, dead, be-

longs to her once more, to her alone, a possession which no one can take from her. She writes at once to the Abbot of Cluny for details about the death of her former love, her spouse, her father. These she receives, and it is to the reply of Peter the Venerable that we are indebted for the foregoing facts. His long letter was slow in coming because, he writes, he was overwhelmed by the numerous obligations of his post, but no doubt too by reason of the unusual character of his letter which is certainly addressed beyond Héloïse to posterity itself.

The testimony of Peter the Venerable takes on an inestimable value for us because it is a twelfth-century document on twelfth-century history. Speaking as a man of his day on an affair of his day, he marvelously communicates something of the Christian awareness of an age vastly different from our own. As a test of this difference, let us imagine a parallel case in which, after a public scandal like theirs, two lovers today seek refuge in the religious life. Making allowance for changes in custom, the case is not absolutely impossible. They live out their days in penance within the silence of the cloister. But what happens when one of them dies? Probably nothing, save that the other would likely be sent the sad news and asked to pray for the repose of the soul of the departed sinner. As for the rest, why talk about it? Why open old sores? Why, above all, revive a scandal better buried in oblivion?

Peter the Venerable proceeds rather differently. He does not pretend not to know what everybody else knows. He sees that the great lesson their exemplary penance has for the world will be lost unless their sin too is known; and the depth of their sin is inextricably bound to the stature of the

sinners. Thus he accepts as real both the sinners and their
expiation. He accepts Héloïse herself, her letters, even the
gifts she had sent on beforehand, in grateful acknowledg-
ment of the haven he provided for the man she loved. The
abbot treats the abbess, as a friend whom he loves in Christ,
with a ready ease that brings to life for us the actors in this
drama. What Héloïse and Abélard thought of each other,
Peter the Venerable thinks too, as indeed, one quickly realizes, did everyone else concerned. Thanks to his testimony,
the fictional elements in the story become less acceptable,
the real elements more so. His is the seal of authenticity.

Héloïse he has admired from his youth. At the very moment of solemn decision not to keep them separated, his
first thoughts are of the splendid young girl of a few short
years ago: "My affection for you does not begin today, but
dates from a long way back. I was scarcely more than a
boy, hardly a young man, when the renown, not yet of your
religious life, but of your noble and praiseworthy studies
reached me. Men were speaking of this wonder—a woman,
still in the world, giving herself entirely to the study of
literature and philosophy, nor permitting anything, neither
the desires of the world, nor its vanities, nor its pleasures to
turn her from the laudable ambition of learning the liberal
arts." Héloïse's youthful fame is no fabrication of history.
In an era when studies interested no one—Peter's remarks
fit any and every age—when not only women were completely indifferent to wisdom, but when men as well lacked
courage to pursue it, Héloïse "surpassed all women and
most men". Before long, however, she whom God wanted
for His own, was exchanging her logic for the Gospels, her
physics for St. Paul, Plato for Christ, the Academy for the

Cloister. Then, indeed, was she becoming a true philosopher. Peter is judiciously silent about the circumstances of her change, lest he belittle its cause—divine grace, and its effect—the marvelous and exemplary life of an abbess victorious over the devil by the rigor of her penance, and to whose merits were to be added those of all the holy women she was guiding towards salvation.

Could all this be flattery? The abbot says No. In praising Héloïse for a greatness of which she is not conscious, he is showing her precisely in what her greatness consists so that she will be able to conserve it. Once again, Peter's psychology is faultless. He knows that Héloïse will only be saved by an appeal to her courage, to her strength, to her taste for the heroic, to the hidden depths of her nature whence spring her qualities of guide and leader. You are not only a glowing coal, he told her, but a shining lamp. You must illumine as well as be consumed. The Héloïse he knows is made to fight and to lead others into battle. She is Penthesilea, queen of the Amazons, who leads her army of women into the combat. She is Debbora, the prophetess, who rouses the courage of Barac, judge of Israel. "I should like", adds the Abbot of Cluny, "to speak with you at length of these things, because I am pleased by your well-known erudition; and your piety, which many have praised, attracts me even more." What a pity Cluny had no Héloïse! Would that she were enclosed in the pleasant prison of Marcigny, there to await the liberty of heaven with the other servants of Christ! Peter would have preferred the wealth of her learning and piety to the greatest treasures of kings. And Héloïse herself would have admired the virtue of these virgins and widows who were trampling under foot the glories of this world. But indeed her presence in this house could only have enhanced its beauty.

This, alas, has not been in the designs of God. Cluny will never have Héloïse. But, at least, it has had Abélard—"Your Abélard", writes Peter, "that servant of Christ, that true philosopher, whose name will ever be spoken with honor, that Master Pierre whom Divine Providence brought to Cluny in his declining years, enriching it with a treasure more precious than silver and gold". We already know how the learned master, whose fame was spreading throughout the world, ended his days at Saint-Marcel. We have seen him becoming the disciple of Him who said: "Learn of me, for I am meek and humble of heart". Certainly we trust that after such perseverance in meekness and humility, he has moved on towards his Redeemer. "Venerable Sister, he to whom you were joined first in the flesh and then by the stronger and more perfect bond of divine charity, he with whom and under whom you too have served the Saviour, is now sheltered in the bosom of Christ. Christ now protects him in your place, indeed as a second you, and will restore him to you on that day when He returns from the heavens between the voice of the archangel and the sounding trumpet."

How well Peter the Venerable knew Héloïse! "What psychologists!" remarked Lucien Lévy-Bruhl one day to a group of us as we stood entranced before the statues of the Great Portal of Chartres. And the Abbot of Cluny was of their century and their race. But perhaps it is charity alone that has intuition and understanding to a degree like this. No calculation, no premeditated design could have inspired so surprising a remark, baffling indeed to the

learned calculations of theological speculation, but revealing, nevertheless, the sure and steady touch of the genuine
master: "Christ is sheltering him, I say, in His bosom in
your place, as a second you."[5] He was a God whom this
abbess, confounded, rebellious, walled up, as it were, in her
sorrow, could hardly refuse to love. Indeed it was He Who
was guarding her Abélard for her, for her and in her very
place—*ut te alteram*—that one day He might restore him
to her forever.

This is the end. Héloïse has nothing further to say, but
much to do. So long as she can be busy looking after Abélard, her task is not done. The mortal remains of her beloved are still far away. And he had asked to be buried, not
at Saint-Marcel, but at the Paraclete. How was she to carry
out this wish? At her request, Peter the Venerable had the
body of Abélard secretly removed from the cemetery of
Saint-Marcel and brought it himself to the Paraclete. This
was the occasion of his first visit to Héloïse and her sisters.
Like the Abbot of Clairvaux before him, the Abbot of
Cluny was amazed by this interview. Héloïse herself must
have guarded its memory. But still she had other things to
put in order. Having got Cluny to surrender the body of
Abélard, she succeeded in getting Peter the Venerable to
promise a benefice and a trental of Masses for the repose of
her soul after her death. She also insisted on sealed letters
confirming the gift of Abélard's body and sealed assurance
that he had received absolution for all his sins.[6] This was
to be suspended above his tomb. When these duties towards Abélard were fulfilled, she remembered too that she
was a mother. She therefore asked the Abbot to do what
he could to find for an unfortunate man some prebend or

other with the bishop of Paris or some other bishop. Thus
Héloïse gets all she asks—the trental, the sealed letters assuring her of the body, and those guaranteeing that Abélard
had received absolution. As for the benefice for their child,
the Abbot replies, it is a more difficult matter. Bishops are
often deaf to requests for prebends; but he will do whatever
he can when the occasion arises.[7] If he had not already
understood it, Peter the Venerable certainly understood
now that in this whole affair there was something to be said
for Abélard's point of view. Héloïse survived her lover by
twenty-one years and died on the sixteenth of May, 1164,
having reached the same age as he. Here history comes to
an end and legend begins. It is told that, shortly before her
death, Héloïse arranged to be buried with Abélard. When
his tomb was opened and her body placed by his, he raised
his arms to receive her and closed them fast about her. The
story, thus related, is beautiful. But matching legend for
legend, we would much prefer to believe that when Héloïse
joined her lover in their tomb, she was the one who opened
her arms for the embrace.

VIII

Conclusion

IN SPITE of the many problems still left unsolved in this history of Héloïse and Abélard, there is sufficient information available to make the effort of gathering it all together quite worth while. There are literally hundreds of definitions of the Renaissance, most of which concur in assigning as its essential characteristic, the appearance of strong individuals capable at last of giving expression to their own personality, after centuries of medieval oppression. There is nothing quite comparable to the passion of the historians of the Renaissance for its individualism, its independence of mind, its rebellion against the principle of authority, unless perchance it is the docility with which those same historians copy one another in dogmatizing about the Middle Ages of which they know so little. We should not attach much importance to this attitude, save that those who speak thus of things they understand so poorly pretend to act in defense of reason and of personal observation. Their charge that all those who hold a different opinion are yielding to prejudice would, indeed, be sad, were it not so comic. Indifference to facts, distrust of direct observation and personal knowledge, the tendency to prune their data to suit their hypotheses, the naïve and dogmatic tendency to charge that those who would refute their position with self-evident facts lack a critical sense—these are the substance of their charge against the Middle Ages. Certainly, the Middle Ages had its fair share of these limitations. But at the same time these same limitations provide a perfect picture of the attitude of these historians of the Renaissance. They themselves possess the weaknesses of which they accuse the Middle Ages.

For Jacob Burckhardt, who only echoes the Preface to Volume VII of Michelet's *History of France*, the Renaissance is characterized by the discovery of the world and by the discovery of man. "To the discovery of the outward world the Renaissance added a still greater achievement by first discerning and bringing to light the full, whole nature of man." Once the principle is stated, the consequences follow of themselves: "This period, as we have seen, first gave the highest development to individuality, and then led the individual to the most zealous and thorough study of himself in all forms and under all conditions."[1] It is therefore the great poets of the fourteenth century whom he first discusses as providing a "free delineation of the human spirit",[2] or as the French translator puts it, "of the moral man", and above all Dante who established a "boundary between medievalism and modern times".[3] It is perhaps true, as Ernest Renan and Pierre de Nolhac say, that Petrarch was the first of the moderns.[4] But what does it matter? Are we for all this any nearer the first modern man? For Burckhardt this is not the essential thing. What he wishes to prove before everything else is that such strong individuals could only have appeared first in the tiny Italian

tyrannies of the fourteenth century where men led so in-
tense a personal life that they had to talk about it. And so
we read that "Even autobiography (and not merely history) takes here and there in Italy a bold and vigorous
flight, and puts before us, together with the most varied
incidents of external life, striking revelations of the inner
man. Among other nations, even in Germany, at the time
of the Reformation, it deals only with outward experiences,
and leaves us to guess at the spirit within. It seems as though
Dante's *La Vita nuova*, with the inexorable truthfulness
that runs through it, had shown his people the way."[5] We
can, moreover, find a reason for this absence of individuality
among medieval folk. Need we speak it? It is to be found
in the subjugation and standardization which Christianity
forced upon them. "Once mistress, the Church does not
tolerate the development of the individual. All must be re-
signed to becoming simple links in her long chain and to
obeying the laws of her institutions."[6]

A man lacking individuality, incapable of analyzing himself, without the taste for describing others in biography or
himself in autobiography, such is the man Christianity produces.[7] Let us cite, as an example, St. Augustine! But to
confine ourselves to the twelfth century, and without asking from what unique mould we could fashion at the same
time a Bernard of Clairvaux and a Pierre Abélard, let us
make a simple comparison between the Renaissance of the
professors and the facts which become manifest in the correspondence of Héloïse and Abélard.

If all we need for a Renaissance is to find individuals developed to the highest point, does not this pair suffice? To
be sure, Abélard and Héloïse are not Italians. They were

not born in some tiny Tuscan "tyranny" of the fourteenth century. They satisfy, in brief, none of the conditions which the theory demands except that they were just what they ought not to have been if the theory were true. One insists, however, upon persons capable of "freely describing the moral man", even as the great Italians could do it. Perhaps even here Abélard and Héloïse labored with some success! No one would be so foolish as to compare their correspondence with the *Vita nuova* as literature. But if it is just a matter of stating in which of the two works one finds the moral man more simply and more directly described, the tables are turned. It is the *Vita nuova* that can no longer bear the comparison. Historians still wonder whether Beatrice was a little Florentine or a symbol. But there is nothing symbolic about Héloïse, nor was her love for Abélard but the unfolding of allegorical remarks. This story of flesh and blood, carried along by a passion at once brutal and ardent to its celebrated conclusion, we know from within as, indeed, we know few others. Its heroes observe themselves, analyze themselves as only Christian consciences fallen prey to passions can do it. Nor do they merely analyze themselves, but they talk about themselves as well. What Renaissance autobiographies can be compared with the correspondence of Abélard and Héloïse? Perchance Benvenuto Cellini's? But even Burckhardt recognizes that this does not claim to be "founded on introspection". Moreover, the reader "often detects him bragging or lying." On the contrary, it is absolutely certain that it is their inmost selves about which Abélard and Héloïse instruct us; and if they sometimes lie to themselves, they never lie to us.

Before such disagreement between facts and theory, we might reasonably expect the theory to yield a little. But not a bit of it! Rather it is here that we reach the crux of the problem. The interpretation of the Renaissance and of the Middle Ages which we now happen to be reading is not at all, as we should like to think, an historical hypothesis warranted by the facts. It is one of those fundamental positions which G. Séailles might have willingly gathered into his *Affirmations de la conscience contemporaine.* There is no discussing such an affirmation. It is not dictated by facts. It proceeds from the conscience; and it is the conscience that dictates the facts. Benvenuto Cellini is not speaking about the moral being; he is guilty of lying on almost every page of his *Autobiography.* But Burckhardt says, what does it matter? "It does not spoil the impression."[8] It is still an Italian autobiography of the fourteenth century, as unchristian as can be. It is just what the professors of the Renaissance say that it should be. Accordingly, it is an autobiography of importance. But Abélard and Héloïse speak only of the moral man, and are they not sincere? Yes, but they are French, Christian, and belong to the twelfth century. They do not conform to the exigencies of the theory. Their correspondence, accordingly, is not important. I am not exaggerating here. I do not really mean that they are forgetting their story, that they neglect to take it into consideration. I mean that they do think about it but that they discard it, as they discard any fact whatsoever that happens to disagree with the principle, which must be maintained at any price. Here, then, we are warned. No fact, whatever it may be, no facts, however numerous they may be, can ever persuade those who hold

this theory that it is false, because it is of its very essence
and by definition that the Renaissance is the negation of
the Middle Ages. "One can find in the Renaissance any
number of mediaeval survivals, pointed arches, mysticism,
mysteries, scholasticism, but one must not lose sight of the
essential in favor of the accessory, forgetting that in the
realm of the mind it represents the liberation of the individual in what concerns dogma."[9]

There are so many who hold views like this that the dawn
of liberation is still a long way off. The best example we
can find of historical cliché is the concept of an anti-Chris-
tian Renaissance which historians of literature pass on from
one to the other as though Lefèvre d'Etaples, Budé, Erasmus, ever pretended to be escaping from any dogma, or
as if their adherence to dogmas ever prevented St. Bernard
from being eloquent, Dante and Petrarch from writing
well, or St. Bonaventure and St. Thomas from thinking.
But none of this carries any weight. Since, as Morf has it,
the Renaissance is an "insurrection against the City of
God",[10] they (the Renaissance historians) will affirm with
Lefranc that "in essence, the Renaissance is a movement of
emancipation supposing a diminution of the Christian ideal;
this is the great change which explains the whole evolution
of literature since the sixteenth century."[11] Or, to take another definition from Lefranc, the Renaissance was an "in-
tellectual laicization of humanity."[12] This definition suggests Combes, now revived by G. Cohen: the Renaissance
is "the separation of Church and Poetry". Perhaps it is not
so much the spirit of Combes but of Aristide Briand that
has penetrated the history of literature.

The consequences of such methods it is not even necessary to imagine. They are right here before our eyes in the books of scholars, ready to be poured out freely into students' manuals. When the principle is stated, facts must retreat. Since Rabelais is a Renaissance figure, and since the Renaissance is pagan, therefore Rabelais was necessarily an atheist. This conclusion may demand certain misinterpretations, but it will stand none the less.[13] But there is something even more comical than this. Let us suppose for a moment that we have an historian of infinite good will, one not at all wedded to the notion of literary laicization, but quite convinced of the common opinion that the concept of Renaissance is inseparable from that of a return to Hellenism. Such a one will find scarcely any Hellenism in Montaigne. Therefore he will be tempted to remove him from the Renaissance; and thus at the very moment when the Renaissance gains the atheist Rabelais, it loses the theologian Montaigne.[14] Let this kind of thing go on for a while, and we shall soon have a Middle Ages peopled with Humanists and a Renaissance that has become the golden age of scholastic theology—a change of setting both picturesque and comic.

To escape from this confusion, it might be well to remember that the expressions *Middle Ages* and *Renaissance* are abstract symbols for otherwise ill-defined chronological periods. There is no hope that anyone will ever succeed in giving them single definitions, applicable to everything they designate. There has not been an *essence* of the Middle Ages nor of the Renaissance and so neither can ever have a definition. Abélard and St. Bernard lived in the Middle Ages; Romanesque architecture and Gothic architecture belong to it; the *Jesu dulcis memoria*, the *Adoro te devote* and the songs of the Goliards meet therein; while St. Thomas proclaims theology "queen", and even "goddess of the sciences", the Averroists teach "that the only wise men in the world are the philosophers alone, and they know no more about it [theology] for knowing philosophy", and that "the teachings of theology are founded upon fables". What is medieval about all this? It is all medieval: St. Louis and Frederick II, St. Thomas who composed the Office of the Blessed Sacrament and those clerics of the University of Paris who in 1276 had to be restrained from dicing (and from oaths by God, the Blessed Virgin and all the saints which accompany it) on the very altars where daily by the ministry of the priest the Body and Blood of Our Redeemer are consecrated.[15] Which of these things is more medieval than the others? When the young Thomas of Aquin, aged five, became an oblate in the Benedictine Abbey of Monte Cassino, it was assuredly a medieval event which was taking place: "the father of the said brother Thomas made a monk of him as a boy." *(Pater dicti fr. Thomae monachavit eum puerum)*. Could we ask for anything more characteristic of the Middle Ages? But if it was medieval for the father of St. Thomas to "make a monk" of his son at Monte Cassino in 1231, it was no less medieval for Frederick II to expel him from the same monastery in 1239; the insult at Anagni (where Philip IV's envoy seized the aged Pontiff by force in order to bring him back to France for trial) bears the same date [1303] for William of Nogaret who gave it and for Boniface VIII who received it.

If we paid more attention to such evidence, our labor, though not necessarily in complete agreement, would at least lead towards conclusions capable of comparison and consequently of correcting and completing one another. This will not be possible, rather will be impossible, so long as certain historians arrogate to themselves the right to disqualify, in the name of this or that hypothesis, any series of facts whatsoever. Our first problem, therefore, is not to know how many pointed arches or scholastic survivals we can still discover in the time of the Renaissance. Our real concern is to know what a pointed arch is and to be able to recognize a scholastic notion when we meet it. That the historian who meets it should not recognize it, would be of no importance were it not that because he does not recognize it he is led to take it for something else. A real fact; once eliminated, gives place to a feigned fact, created. Then one comments upon it, takes his stand upon it in order to eliminate from history all facts to which this phantom cannot be accommodated. Ronsard belongs to the Renaissance; therefore he must have favored the separation of Church and Poetry. For proof of this, we are offered "the Epicurean and Lucretian formula" with which he closes the *Élégie contre les Bûcherons de la Forêt de Gastine: La matière demeure et la forme se perd*[16] (The matter remains and the form is lost).

In what this formula is either Epicurean or Lucretian we are not told. Certainly it is no more or less so than that of Bernardus Sylvestris when, in the twelfth century, he wrote: *Res eadem subjecta manet, sed forma vagatur* (The subject remains the same, but the form is lost).[17]

Actually, Ronsard is but using the doctrine, classical among all Aristotelians, of the incorruptibility of matter: "Prime matter is not subject to generation or corruption."[18]

But if matter is corruptible, natural form is not. As the Jesuit, Toledo, says in his *Commentary on the Physics of Aristotle* (I, 7, 17): There will be just as much at the end, because it is not subject to generation or corruption. Indeed, there is no generation or corruption except from the point of view of form. So it is that a given matter now under one form can have been hitherto under many forms and will be successively under many more forms." All that Aristotle, St. Thomas, Toledo, and, let us rest assured, Ronsard mean is that when you burn an oak from the forest of Gastine, what remains is not wood but ashes. The form of the wood is lost, but the matter remains under a different form: and to this is reduced the Epicureanism and Lucretianism of Ronsard, Toledo, St. Thomas and Aristotle. Ronsard's verse is only one more vaulted arch in a sixteenth-century Greek temple. There are lots more of them; hence this fact is of interest only to professors of literature, anxious to understand the texts they teach. But it becomes very important, on the contrary, from the moment when, because it has not been recognized for what it is, someone asserts that it is something else and sets out to build upon so ruinous a foundation. It becomes then the case of the Commentary on the Mistranslation, or "the devil in history." In vain does Ronsard give evidence of all sorts, think like a Christian, write like a Christian. It counts for nothing. He cannot be one, he has not the right to have ever been one. The least one can say is that his Christianity is greatly suspect: "It certainly seems, apart from his respect, exterior rather than fundamental, traditionalist rather than spontaneous, for the teachings of the Church, that he was inclined towards the Epicurean metaphysics which old

Lucretius taught him."[19] Thus to assure themselves of the separation of Church and Poetry in the past, our historians become father confessors.

No text seems better able to give a due sense of the complexity of these problems to those anxious to acquire it than the correspondence of Héloïse and Abélard. As Nordström rightly says: "If we had only these precious documents to reveal the penetrating and realistic power of autoanalysis in a medieval man, they would be adequate to demonstrate the fundamental error of Burckhardt when he tells us that Dante was the first to reveal frankly the mysteries of his interior life and thus inaugurate a new epoch in the history of the development of the European man."[20] It could not be put better. Only let us add that if Abélard is a fatal obstacle to Burckhardt's thesis, Héloïse is in her own right a far more dangerous one, not so much because of the passionate ardor with which she analyzes herself, nor of the defiant air with which she publishes her most intimate secrets, but because of the ideas she expresses and the very content of what she says.

Abélard himself was perplexed by it. When he got her to cease her impassioned charges of cruelty against God and of egotism against her lover, she only agreed to be silent about these things in order to go on to speak of others. One nail drives out another,[21] she told him, and so new thoughts drive out old. Héloïse's new subject seemed quite harmless. The Abbess of the Paraclete wanted to know from Abélard first, the story of the origin and dignity of sisterhoods, secondly, what rule, in his opinion, she should impose upon her nuns. A natural question, certainly, for an abbess to ask. But she went on herself to outline an answer; and there are a number of points in this answer which historians of the Renaissance would do well to think about.

First, Héloïse observes, it is a fact that we are without a rule. There is only one rule for monasteries of men and women—the Rule of St. Benedict, which was written for men. This is clear, since Chapter 55, which describes the clothes to be worn by those professed, mentions only the clothing of men. Nor is this all. The rule speaks of the Abbot as reading the Gospel, intoning the hymn that follows, receiving pilgrims and guests at his table. Should an abbess really invite men in this way, share her meal with them, drink with them? What disaster for souls lurks behind such meetings of men and women! Above all at table, where "wine is drunk in enjoyment, wherein is luxury!" (*et vinum in dulcedine bibitur, in quo est luxuria*). This is the teaching of St. Jerome. But it is also the teaching of the poet of luxury and the doctor of indecency in his book entitled *De arte amandi*. Here we have the Abbess of the Paraclete bringing *The Art of Loving* to the support of St. Jerome: "When wine has come to moisten the thirsty wings of Cupid, he alights and remains tightly caught on the place he has picked out.... Then laughter comes; then the wretch imagines he has horns of plenty; then pain disappears and cares too, and the wrinkles from the brow. . . . There the heart of the young man has often fallen victim to the fair; Venus after wine is fire added to fire."[22] Either the abbess had a good memory, which is most likely, or there was a copy of *The Art of Loving* at the Paraclete. Whatever the case, Héloïse hastens to add that to authorize the abbess to receive only women will not meet the situation, for no one knows better than a woman how to corrupt another woman.

Therefore, this article of the rule cannot be observed. But not to fulfill all the obligations of the rule is to violate it entirely. From all this, it would appear that no convent of Benedictine nuns is in a position to keep the rule of religious profession.[23]

Moreover, what is this rule of their profession? It is better perhaps here to let Héloïse herself speak. "Can anything be more absurd than to set out over an unknown route when no one has shown you the way? Is there anything more presumptuous than to choose and profess a kind of life about which you know nothing, or to take a vow which you cannot keep? If, indeed, discretion is the mother of all virtues, and reason the measure of all goods, who can regard as good and virtuous what accords with neither the one nor the other. When they pass beyond their end and measure, even the virtues, says St. Jerome, ought to be reckoned among the vices. Who does not see that it is totally lacking in reason and discernment to impose burdens without examining first the strength of those on whom they are imposed? Zeal must be regulated by the very constitution of nature."[24] In brief, Héloïse considers it absurd to demand of women what is demanded of men. And she bitterly recalls that she bound herself to this rule without realizing to what she was committing herself.

To what, in her opinion, would it be reasonable to commit herself? Her answer here follows a series of shrewdly calculated steps. She proposes first that religious women should be satisfied to equal Church leaders and clerics in holy orders in continence and abstinence.[25] They might then be expected to keep those obligations which fall upon the secular clergy. But she does not stop here. Why belittle layfolk? Are we to imagine that the life of laymen like Abraham, Jacob, and David was without value, even though they were married! Indeed, if we pay attention to St. Paul's words: "Make not provision for the flesh in its concupiscences" (Rom. 13:14), we shall see that they apply not only to monks, but to all who live in the world.[26] The only difference between the layman and the monk is that the former can live with a woman. He has permission to do so. Beyond this, he enjoys no special privilege, and is bound to the same things as the monk. Or, perchance, are the beatitudes only meant for monks? If so, the whole world would be lost and Christ would have planted the virtues in a very narrow field! If marriage were such an obstacle to salvation, it would hardly have deserved respect. And here we are at the point where Héloïse would bring us. The state of monastic perfection adds *nothing more than* continence to the precepts of the Gospel: "Whoever adds the virtue of continence to the Commandments fulfills monastic perfection."[27] In other words, to bring themselves to fulfilling the Gospel, let alone surpassing it, would be itself a very high degree of the religious life for women: "Let us not aspire to be more than Christians."[28]

This is a surprising statement, one, in fact, that brings us in one stride over a space of three centuries. "Would that our religious life achieved this," says Héloïse, "that it fulfilled the Gospel, and did not go beyond it, lest we aspire to be more than Christians." Herein is to be found all that is essential, all that is basic in the criticism of monastic observances of which Erasmus was later to deliver himself. What Héloïse has said for monasteries of religious women applies only too evidently in spirit to those of monks. To

suppose the contrary, it would be necessary to make her say
that St. Paul was only speaking to men and that, although it
was forbidden to women, men at least could legitimately
aspire to a perfection higher than evangelical perfection.
Let us read after this the famous Colloquy of Erasmus,
"The Franciscan", and we will find repeated all the essential ideas of Héloïse: Christ preached but one religion,
the same for layfolk and monks; the Christian renounces
the world and professes to live only for Christ, and St. Paul
did not preach this doctrine for monks but for everyone;
layfolk, even the married, are bound to chastity and poverty quite as much as monks; in short, the only rule binding
the Christian is the Gospel.[29]

Once she has adopted this course, Héloïse's frank and
direct reason would not let her stop. Carried away by her
own logic she was to touch, one after the other, almost all
the critical points on which the humanists and reformers
of the sixteenth century are so insistent. Why forbid meat
to monks? Meat in itself is neither good nor bad. Let us
not attach religious importance to things which in fact have
none.[30] Nothing counts save what can lead us to the king-
dom of God. Let us forget, then, these exterior practices
common to truly pious souls and to hypocrites, It is only
interior acts that really count for the Christian. The rest
is Judaism. After all, has not Christianity substituted the
law of faith for the law of works? As St. Augustine himself says in his *De bono conjugali:* "works add nothing to
merits."[31] The Abélardian theology of intention had only
recently substantiated this criticism of monastic Judaism
and of the superstition of works, whence Héloïse boldly
concludes, *whatever their works,* men of equal virtue will

be treated alike before God.[32] At a time when so many people are blindly rushing into monastic life, professing a Rule which they do not know and assuming burdens they cannot bear,[33] Héloïse ventures to tell them that they run the risk of breaking a vow which will be without merit to observe.

What is her authority for all this criticism? She cites it: "discretion", "reason". It is the teaching of St. Paul, St. Augustine, and St. Jerome (but it is also Seneca's) that we must not trouble ourselves about external things, that is, things "that are outside and said to be indifferent."[34] Thus Héloïse is faithful to the end to the masters whom Abélard had taught her to respect. She even followed them much further than Abélard ever dared, for she was far from obtaining from the man she loved a complete release from the fearful burden she had once assumed and was still bearing to obey him. Héloïse may have ceased to believe in the virtue of monastic observances, but Abélard could never bring himself to release her from any penance which might well be imposed on a pious and poor laywoman. He demanded of Héloïse not only continence, but the most extreme poverty, a perpetual and absolute silence, no excessive use of signs, the common life for all, including the abbess, the Church ornaments as poor and a chapel as bare as St. Bernard would have them, rising during the night to sing the office, and finally, so as to maintain order in the monastery, a strict system of informing on one another, backed up by corporal punishment. For it is written (Prov. 26:3): the whip for the horse, the cord for the ass, and the rod for the back of the imprudent.[35] All this we find, embellished with quotations from Lucan, Ovid and by one from Seneca, surprising, perhaps, in view of what we have just read. Seneca, "that eminent apostle of poverty and continence and supreme master of ethics among all the philosophers, says in *Letter V, to Lucilius*, that our end is to live according to nature. Now it is against nature to torture one's body, to hate easy conveniences, to seek what is dirty, to use food not only spoiled but infected and repugnant." "Philosophy demands frugality, not torture," (*Frugalitatem exigit philosophia non poenam*), says Seneca, as cited by Abélard. Some, at least, of these Senecan modifications mentioned by Héloïse are going to lighten the rule as observed in the Paraclete.

After all, what is sin? It is acting against our conscience. And the testimony of conscience is enough to condemn or absolve a man in the sight of God. In what concerns eating and drinking let everyone follow his conscience, as the Apostle recommends. Nothing we can eat, without giving scandal to ourselves or others, is forbidden. To satisfy nature's need without falling into sin is the real rule. Thus, no imprudent vows, meat once a day, foods of moderate cost, simply prepared, the same fasts as those for layfolk, no exaggeration anywhere. Abélard, like Héloïse, would have discretion, mother of all virtues, preside over the religious life. Let each see what he is capable of imposing upon himself, and let him impose it, "*following* nature, not dragging her along."[36] The "follow nature" of Seneca does not mean for Abélard all that is was to mean for Erasmus, but it is already there, applied by both Abélard and Héloïse to monastic observances, big with all the consequences which are one day to issue from it.

What, then, do the facts teach? That Abélard was the

first of the moderns? This would be to substitute one piece of foolishness for another. That Héloïse was the first modern woman? On the contrary, as Jean de Meung would say, the world has never since seen her like:

> Mais je ne crei mie, par m'ame,
> Qu'onques puis fust nul tel fame.
>
> (By my soul, I do not believe
> That another like her ever lived.)

We should be quite content with a great deal less. We should be content if at the moment they contracted the Middle Ages or the Renaissance into one of their cherished and brilliant definitions, the historians of literature would remember this foolish little Frenchwoman who was haunted by the double ideal of Roman and Christian greatness. She was never quite sure whether she was the Eustochium of a new St. Jerome or the Cornelia of a second Pompey. But she took the veil at Argenteuil for the love of a man and consecrated herself permanently to God with verses from the *Pharsalia* on her lips. Let them remember, too, that this impassioned drama played by clerics and monks and nuns is very much a story of the twelfth century. It can be read as a Christian story because, in very truth, it is one. Héloïse knows Latin, Greek, and Hebrew, studies Scripture and theology, calls on the *Consolation* and the *Exhortations* like the spiritual daughters of St. Jerome before her and because Eustochium, Paula, and Asella had done so too. We shall never know to what extent the ambition to rival by her penances the reputation for continence of these

heroines of the spiritual life helped Héloïse to live so long
and so perfectly in a state for which she did not feel she
had the grace. But Jerome himself is full of Seneca, and
this great saint inspires her with respect for Stoicism. As
the Augustinian theology of intention comments on and
justifies the Stoic disdain of *indifferentia*, we cannot be sure
what spiritual forces prevail in this battle in which monastic
observances are at stake and which so directly menaces an
institution so typically medieval. Why is Héloïse so scorn-
ful of the demands of the monastic rule? Because, as she has
St. Paul put it, it is sheer Judaism. Because, as she has Seneca
say, all these questions of clothing, drink and food belong
with the *indifferentia*, on which wise men do not make wisdom depend. Héloïse coolly writes such things in the heart
of the twelfth century, in the cell of the Abbess of the Paraclete, in the name of prudence and of reason, "mother of
all virtues". But this new Paula belongs also to Romance.
She is the new Cornelia preparing the way for the new
Héloïse. For is not Lucan, too, full of Stoicism? And are
not the characters of the *Pharsalia* quite comprehensible to
one whose very soul was fashioned by Seneca? Like Héloïse, Cornelia had been Pompey's mistress before marrying
him; at least, Julia's shade makes this accusation.[37] Like
Héloïse, Cornelia destroys the hero whom she adores. "O
Spouse, accursed am I that have been Thy undoing."[38] If
Héloïse was in a position to read, in any source whatsoever,
Plutarch's *Life of Pompey*,[39] she would have known that
Cornelia was much more learned than most women of her
time, had studied literature, knew geometry, and had followed with profit the teachings of the philosophers. More-
over, Pompey was reproached for marrying a woman too

young for him, and for letting his marriage distract him from the cares of public life. Which of these stories is here in question? Does the Abbess of Paraclete think she has been the cause of the fall of Pompey? Is it Cornelia who has destroyed Abélard? The one is as true as the other, because Héloïse is Cornelia, and Paula, and Asella even as her Abélard is at once Seneca and St. Jerome. Is this surprising in a story where, even for St. Jerome, Seneca the philosopher is an admirer of St. Paul?

Such are the facts. Before attempting to define the Middle Ages, we should have first to define Héloïse. Next, we should have to look for a definition of Petrarch. This done, we should still have to find a definition of Erasmus. These problems resolved, we might with some confidence seek out our larger definition of the Middle Ages and the Renaissance. But three plus two make five impossibilities. Those who have no taste for undertakings of this kind will be content with the reading and analyzing of texts. Like explorers in an unknown country, they will do nothing more than keep the daily record of their trip. All about the narrow furrow which they plough, behind and beyond what they see to the right and to the left extends the vast territory which they cannot see. But others, too, pass or will pass that way. And when their paths cross and recross one another, not only will each explorer be able to see more, but he will see in a far juster light the few things which he already knows. Before reality, perceived in all its ordered complexity, who will stop to worry about formulas? It is not to be rid of history that we study it, but to save from nothingness the whole past which would be swallowed up without it. We study history so that even those things which otherwise would be lost even from the past may once again come to life in this all-important present, apart from which nothing really exists. In order that this particular human story may live anew in all its individual and concrete complexity, it is enough that we know it. In order that it may enrich us with its very substance, it is enough that we love it.

Appendix

The Authenticity of the Correspondence Between Héloïse and Abélard

THE problem of the authenticity of the correspondence attributed to Héloïse and Abélard is not new. As early as 1841, Orelli attributed the composition of this collection, "for many reasons", to a friend and admirer of the two lovers who, he said, wrote up these letters after their death.[1] Unfortunately, as Orelli says nothing about the numerous reasons leading him to this conclusion, it is impossible to discuss them. On the other hand, we know very well the reasons which made Ludovic Lalanne maintain, in 1857, that the collection of letters attributed to the two lovers gave evident signs of later reworkings. Lalanne's conclusions are less radical than Orelli's[2] but have the merit of being debatable because they are based on precise arguments, or, at least, on arguments among which there is one precise enough to be capable of discussion. Here it is, reduced to its simplest form, but accurately summarized: According to the *Historia calamitatum*, an entirely trustworthy account, Abélard returned from Saint-Gildas de Rhuys to the Paraclete to install Héloïse there. Accordingly, he saw Héloïse again; and Héloïse certainly saw him again when the Benedictine sisters were installed in the

Paraclete in 1129. Now in Héloïse's first letter replying to the *Historia calamitatum,* she expressly states that she has not seen Abélard since the two of them had entered religion. "Tell me at least, if you can, why, *since our conversion,* which you alone decided upon, you have so neglected me, so forgotten me that I have had neither your presence to cheer me up nor even, in your absence, a letter to console me." Whence Lalanne's conclusion: "Even supposing, and this is very difficult to admit, that Héloïse had not seen Abélard again from the time of his misfortune to the moment when, chased from Argenteuil, she was received into the Paraclete in 1129, it is nevertheless a fact that in this last period she did see him. How then can she complain that, from her entrance into religion; that is, after 1119 or 1120, she had not been able to obtain either his presence or a single letter? And she was writing this in 1133 or 1134! I am unable to believe that it was she who wrote these lines."[3]

Neither Lalanne's arguments nor his conclusion seem to have given rise to any controversy.[4] In 1913, B. Schmeidler took them up again for his own purpose and added new arguments.[5] Still more recently, Charlotte Charrier took over and completed in her turn Schmeidler's arguments. She has done this with such success that Lalanne's thesis, after years of neglect, is today taken as historical criticism's last word on the question.[6]

Such success is far from deserved. But since Lalanne has finally succeeded in finding disciples, the question must be taken up once more. We should like to do this in the following pages, discussing his thesis in the highly refined form in which Schmeidler and Miss Charrier have presented it.

Tedious as such discussions are, the stake in this case is worth the trouble spent on it. For according as we accept or reject the authenticity of this remarkable document, our view not only of Héloïse and Abélard but of the twelfth century itself is affected.

The first argument which was passed on from Lalanne to Schmeidler and from Schmeidler to Miss Charrier, we have already summarized: The *Historia calamitatum*, point of departure for the Correspondence, cannot have been written before 1132, since it mentions a privilege of Pope Innocent II which we know was given to the Paraclete, November 28, 1131. In addition, since Abélard speaks of the long persecutions endured at Saint-Gildas, the *Historia* can only have been written between the end of 1132 and the year 1134. Abélard tells us in this work how, after the expulsion of the religious from Argenteuil, he returned from Saint-Gildas to the Paraclete to install Héloïse and several of her companions. Certainly, on this occasion, he saw Héloïse again. This one fact makes Héloïse's first letter to Abélard impossible, because in it she states in two places that, "since the two of them had entered religion" *(seit sie beide ins Kloster getreten sind)*, she has not seen Abélard again in person, nor received any letter from him. We have to choose between the *Historia calamitatum* and Héloïse's letter. It cannot possibly be true both that Abelard installed Héloïse in the Paraclete as the *Historia* says, and that Héloïse did not see Abélard again, as it says in her first letter to him. Now the authority of the *Historia calamitatum* is unimpeachable. Therefore Héloïse's letter is false.[7]

Schmeidler's arguments are based on two essential texts

(on the second of which Lalanne also relied) and which he cites from Victor Cousin's version.[8]

1. Unde non mediocri admiratione nostrae tenera conversionis initia tua iam dudum oblivio movit, quod nec reverentia Dei, nec amore nostri, nec sanctorum patrum exemplis admonitus, fluctuantem me et iam diutino moerore confectam vel sermone praesentem vel epistola absentem consolari tentaveris.

2. Dic unum, si vales, cur post conversionem nostram, quam tu solus facere decrevisti, in tantam tibi negligentiam atque oblivionem venerim, ut nec colloquio praesentis recreer, nec absentis epistola consoler: dic, inquam, aut ego quod sentio, imo quod omnes suspicantur dicam . . . etc.

If it is necessary to explain how our modern critics have come to understand these texts in the sense they do, the reason probably lies in the manner in which Lalanne translated the second text.[9] Lalanne himself is later than Oddoul, and Oddoul's translation might well lie behind it all. It runs as follows: "Only tell me, if you can, why, since our entrance into religion which you resolved upon without consulting me, you have so neglected me, so forgotten me, that it has not been given me to have either your presence to renew my courage or even a letter to enable me to endure your absence."[10] Octave Gréard in his elegant and often happy translation of the letters in question, takes the same passage in an analagous manner: "Tell me only, if you can, why since my retreat which you alone decided upon, you have come to neglect me, to forget me so much that it has not been given me either to hear you in order to renew my courage, or to read you to console myself for your absence . . . ."[11] Miss Charrier, who generally follows Gréard, replaces the familiar form of address, which he uses, by the more dignified and conventional form, but keeps the rest of his translation.[12] The wrong shade of meaning taken by Oddoul, repeated by Lalanne, then by Gréard, taken again by Schmeidler and meekly accepted by Miss Charrier is, as we shall see, the source of the difficulty.[13]

Let us note first that this second text does not say "my retreat" as Gréard and Miss Charrier would have it, but rather "our retreat"—*conversionem nostram.* Oddoul translates it "our entrance into religion": Héloïse's to Argenteuil, Abélard's to Saint-Denys. It might be maintained that Héloïse is here using the plural of excellence; but were she doing so the verbs which follow ought normally also to be in the plural. They are actually in the singular: *venerim, recreer, consoler.* She is, then, certainly speaking of *their* entrance into religion and "our retreat" is the only correct translation of the passage.

Next let us observe—and this point is equally important— that neither Oddoul, nor Gréard, nor Miss Charrier have, in their translations, hesitated to put into the perfect subjunctive two verbs which appear in the present subjunctive in the Latin text. *Recreer, consoler* cannot be translated: "*it has not been given to me* either to hear you . . . or to read you . . .*"; but rather: "*it is not given to me* either to hear you . . . or to read you." But if we correct the translation in this way, we are going to get a rather awkward phrase: "*since* our retreat, it *is* not given to me." Clearly, *since* calls for a past tense. Accordingly, Oddoul, Gréard and Miss Charrier, one after the other, have spontaneously used the past tense of the verbs which follow. They have an excuse for so doing, but no reason, because *post* in Latin can mean either *since*, or merely *after*, according to the tense of the verb which follows. In Héloïse's phrase *post conversionem nostram, etc.*, the normal sense appears indeed to be: after our common entrance into religion, which you alone decided upon, you abandon me to the point, etc. On the other hand, in his reply to this very phrase, Abélard writes: "quod *post* nostram a saeculo ad Deum conversionem nondum tibi aliquid consolationis vel exhortationis *scripserim* . . .";[14] which means, this time, that *since* their common entrance into religion, Abélard has written Héloïse no letter of consolation or exhortation;[15] but Abélard does not say that he has not seen Héloïse since their religious profession. In fact, he says the contrary (191B). Each phrase must therefore be interpreted for itself, and the one whose sense we are seeking means simply: after our entrance into religion, which you alone decided upon, I am so deserted and forgotten that I have neither your presence nor your words to revive my courage, nor a letter from you to console me for your absence. Between this text properly translated and the *Historia calamitatum*, there appears to be no contradiction. Héloïse is not complaining of having never seen Abélard, but of his absence which was a fact, and of receiving no letter of consolation or direction, which was another fact. The problem vanishes as soon as the rules of grammar are applied.

There still remains the first text, *Epist.* II c. 184B, where Héloïse does use a past tense—*tentaveris*. Gréard translates: "nothing has inspired you with the thought of coming to strengthen me by your discourse, or at least console me from afar by a letter." If *nostrae conversionis* in this case also signifies "our religious profession, yours at Saint-Denys, mine at Argenteuil", it is obvious that by accusing Abélard of never having come to see her at the Paraclete, Héloïse is contradicting the *Historia calamitatum*, and that one or other of these texts has no historical value. But it is not at all clear that this is the meaning of *nostrae conversionis*. In their context, these words can also mean the *conversio* of Héloïse and some of her religious who followed her to the Paraclete, that is, the beginning of their monastic life at the Paraclete, quite as well as the religious profession of Héloïse and Abélard. Translators and critics have been turned aside from this meaning, which the context calls for, by the fact that the word *conversio* naturally suggests entrance into religion, and that it moreover has this very meaning later on in 186B: "our entrance into religion which you alone insisted upon". The two passages seem parallel. Since *conversio* means entrance into religion in the second, why should it mean anything different in the first? Neither Héloïse nor her sisters took the veil at the Paraclete, but at Argenteuil. Since, this time, the verb actually is in the past tense—*tentaveris*—it follows that Héloïse would not have seen Abélard at all after taking the veil. This contradicts the *Historia calamitatum* and Abélard's actual reply.

We can reply to this that *conversio* means not only "religious profession" but also "monastic life". In all the ancient Benedictine texts the two words *conversio* and *conversatio* are practically interchangeable. So true is this that in the critical editions of the *Rule*, almost everywhere the word *conversatio* appears in the text, *conversio* is to be found among the variants. It is useless to repeat here the reasons for this as discussed and interpreted by Dom C. Butler.[16] But we must point out the delicate distinction of meaning which has produced this interchange between the two words. *Conversatio*, in the Pauline sense,[17] suggests the state or even the rule of the monastic life. *Conversio* suggests rather the act of entering into monastic life either by taking the veil or by religious profession. Actually either word can have either meaning, but their normal meanings are the ones indicated. We need not go outside the correspondence of Héloïse and Abélard in order to illustrate this double meaning:

119A: *suae conversionis habitus:* G. de Champeaux enters the Canons Regular of Saint-Victor. Whereupon Hildebert, bishop of Le Mans, writes to him: "*de conversione et conversatione tua laetabitur . . . anima mea*". (118, note 17).

134A: *vestes quoque ei (Heloissae) religionis, quae conversioni,* [al. *conversationi*] *monasticae convenirent:* André Duchesne hesitated over the correct reading; here, it is evidently *conversationi.*

136A: *devotio conversionis:* the act of vowing oneself to the religious life; normal use of *conversio.*

186C: *monasticae conversationis asperitatem:* the rigour of the religious life; *conversationis* was to be expected.

213C: *nostrae conversationis* [al. *conversionis* and *professionis*] *statum:* Duchesne hesitates again; *conversationis* is correct.

218C: *ad monasticam conversationem* [al. *conversionem*] *currentes:* the same case; *conversationem* is the better reading.

257D: *vestram instruere conversationem:* your religious life at the Paraclete.

258D: *Hanc autem ad Deum spiritalem a saeculo conver-*

sionem: this spiritual conversion which turns you away from the world and towards God.

If we add to these examples the whole series of texts in which *conversio* clearly means "entrance into religion",[18] it becomes obvious that this is the usual meaning of the term. *Conversatio,* on the contrary stands, in the language of Abélard and Héloïse, for the monastic state of life. Neither Gréard nor Miss Charrier were wrong in giving to *conversio* the meaning "religious profession", for this, indeed, is its true meaning. But Miss Charrier was wrong in establishing her critical work on this meaning of the word without first being certain that the word was in the text. For indeed it is not there. Of the four oldest manuscripts, three agree in giving in all the letters *conversacionis* for the text 184B, and, on the other hand, *conversionem* for 186B.[19] There is no doubt that in both cases the reading of these manuscripts is sound. Duchesne and Cousin would have done well to follow it. Duchesne was much at fault for not at least indicating hesitation about the reading. *Nostrae tenera conversationis initia* certainly means: "the still fragile beginnings of the religious life" which we are leading here in the Paraclete.

It is sufficient merely to put the text thus re-established back into its context, from which it ought never to have been taken, in order to be reassured in the whole matter. Héloïse is complaining that Abélard has written his *Historia calamitatum* for a friend, while he leaves her and the religious of the Paraclete without a word. Now we, she tells him, are not just your friends, nor even your very great friends *(amicissimas)*, nor your companions *(socias)*, we are your daughters. If you have a moment's doubt as to your obligations towards them *(erga eas)*, you need only consider the facts. You, after God, are the sole founder of this house *(hujus loci)*, and the sole builder of this congregation *(solus hujus congregationis aedificator)*. Whatever is here, you have created, both buildings and oratory. The entire plantation is yours and the tender plants still claim your assiduous care: "This new plantation is, in its holy plan, properly yours. It is filled for the most part with plants that are still tender, and it needs watering *(Tua haec est proprie in sancto proposito novella plantatio, cujus adhuc teneris maxime plantis frequens . . . necessaria est irrigatio)*." Besides, it is a question of women, and the weakness of their sex alone explains the weakness of this foundation: "It would be weak, even if it were not new *(est infirma, et si non esset nova)*." You are losing your time at Saint-Gildas de Rhuys cultivating another's vineyard rather than your own: "You, who are so generous towards your enemies, consider what you owe to your daughters *(quid filiabus debeas meditare)*. To say nothing of the others, think at least of the debt which you have contracted to me. In this way, what you owe to all these holy women, you will acquit all the more holily towards her who is yours in so unique a manner. How many long and serious treatises the holy Fathers composed, and with what care, in order to instruct, exhort or even to console holy women, you in your excellence know far better than we in our lowly estate. Moreover, have not the still frail first fruits of our religious community been for a good while[20] rather surprised that neither out of respect for God nor love for us, nor to follow the example of the holy Fathers, have you tried either to come and console me with your discourse or to write to me from

afar when I am staggering in exhaustion under such penetrating sorrow" (col. 183B-184B).

We could scarcely demand more consistency in what is
after all only a letter, however studied it may be. Abélard
is dutybound to write to his daughters of the Paraclete. Let
him acquit this duty in the person of their abbess who is not
only his daughter, like all the others, but his wife, and the
possessor of unique rights over him. The second letter reproduces the same trend of thought. "Tell me, if you can,
why after *our* entrance into religion which you alone decided upon *(post conversionem nostram, quam tu solus
facere decrevisti)*, I find myself so neglected and forgotten
that I have not the encouragement of your discourse and
your presence nor, in your absence, the consolation of a
letter. Tell me this if you can; or I will tell you what I
think about it all, and what, moreover, everybody else sus-
pects" (col. 186B). Here it is clearly a question of conversion in the sense of entrance into religion; hence the
same fourteenth-century manuscripts read *conversionem*.[21]
Héloïse does not let go of her idea. Both arguments hold
out for the same thing: you have placed us all here in the
Paraclete and you do not so much as write to your daughters in the person of their abbess. You forced me into religion and you are now leaving me without direction. If
either one of these arguments works, Héloïse will have the
letters she is looking for.

If this is the true meaning of these passages, the principal
objection to the historicity of the Correspondence is reduced to what are only too often the discoveries of historical criticism—a commentary on a misconstruction. When
he has made an initial error, the modern critic is capable of

the most ingenious findings to remove the many obstacles
he is so certain to run up against. All texts must strengthen
his thesis, even those which actually weaken it. Thus we
have already cited the text of Epist. III where Abélard admits that he has never written a word of consolation or
exhortation to Héloïse since their entrance into religion.
Schmeidler concludes from this that the whole letter is
spurious because he finds its beginning so. Then he per-
ceives that in fact Abélard is only accusing himself of not
having written to Héloïse, not of not having come to see
her, so that no contradiction exists between *Epist. III* and
the *Historia calamitatum.* To avoid this misfortune, in
the same note in which he proves his argument invalid,
Schmeidler presents it under a second form: "If the letter
had really been written by Abélard, in reply to the second
letter which he would really have received, he would not
have been able to explain himself as above, but would have
had to write something like this: 'How can you reproach
me in this way? I have, indeed, gone to see you often, with
the result that evil rumors have gone round about me!' "[22]
Hence the result, first, that for a letter to be Abélard's, it
is not enough that Abélard should have written it, but it is
necessary that he should have written it as Schmeidler
would have done in his place; secondly, that while Héloïse
was reproaching Abélard for having never written her,
logic would have Abélard reply: why should I write you,
when I have gone to see you. It is unfortunate that
Schmeidler did not rewrite all these love letters as Héloïse
and Abélard ought to have written them so that one day
they might be shown to be authentic. "Wie kannst du mir
überhaupt solche Vorwürfe machen, ich bin doch sehr

oft bei Dir gewesen. . . ." This is not just logic, it is really quite charming.

Beginning at this point, that is, by supposing that Abélard would have said or ought to have said something which in fact he never said, all sorts of arguments against the authenticity of the Correspondence can be gathered together. Hence, Schmeidler and his French prophet have trumped up the following.

1. Abélard reminds Héloïse that when he was at the Paraclete, the sisters used to pray for him every day; he is sending them new prayers to recite. But all this is unacceptable. "The same man who began his letter by unscrupulously admitting that he had never been concerned about his wife since the two of them had entered the convent, now writes and reminds her in the same letter that he has been with the sisters in the cloister of the Paraclete and that they have prayed for him."[23] What could be more contradictory!—Certainly, it would have been contradictory if Abélard had actually said that he had not seen Héloïse nor been concerned about her since their entrance into religion. But he did not say it, and there is no contradiction.

2. Abélard protests, in Letter III, against Héloïse's old, stubborn complaint about God's injustice towards them. Since they have neither seen each other nor written, since their entrance into religion, when could he have heard her complaining?[24]—Reply: Abélard heard her complaining at the Paraclete; that is, about three years before, and during at least two years.

3. Another objection based on the same principle: "Still in the first letter, Héloïse speaks, as of something actual, of *the frail beginnings of her conversion.* This expression

sounds exaggerated at the moment at which she is supposed
to be writing, since by then twelve or fifteen years have
passed since she first took her vows."[25]—True, so far as
Argenteuil is concerned; but the text refers to the foundation at the Paraclete, and it was not more than a year and
a half after the monastery was founded when Abélard departed.

4. Abélard promises Héloïse a psalter which she has demanded with some insistence; "now in her letter Héloïse
has not spoken of a psalter. Perhaps, it will be objected, she
demanded it *viva voce?* But she pretends that Abélard and
she have not seen each other again."[26]—Not at all. Héloïse
only claims not to have seen Abélard since his departure
from the Paraclete. When Abélard saw the turn Héloïse's
letters were taking and that she was asking for help and
direction for her daughters, we can easily imagine his re-
calling her request. You can yourself look after your
daughters, is the substance of his remarks to her, for you
have the necessary authority and learning. However, if in
your humility you judge otherwise, and if you need instruction from me or books, write and let me know. But since,
thanks be to God, you are uneasy about me and share my
troubles, ask in your prayers that God in His mercy will
protect me. *Ad hoc autem praecipue* ... : "it is chiefly for
this, Sister, who of old in the world were so dear to me,
and who now in Christ are infinitely dear to me, that I have
hastened to send you the psalter which you have asked me
for with insistence."[27] Why might not Héloïse have asked
insistently for a psalter while Abélard was still with her at
the Paraclete?

5. Fifth objection, and one which will provide us with

the occasion to settle a sixth. "Héloïse, in her first letter, addresses Abélard as if he was still Prior of Saint-Gildas; and Abélard replies as though still directing his rebellious monks. At this date this is impossible since Abélard had already fled from his convent when he wrote the *Historia calamitatum*."[28]—Yes, he had fled, but he had returned after his second departure from the Paraclete. What cloister could he have had in mind, other than that of which he was abbot, when he writes at the end of his letter: "It is in the cloister of my sons, that is, of my monks, for to entrust me to them as their abbot is to entrust them to me as their father, that I am the butt of violence and trickery".[29] He is using the present indicative, and he is clearly among his monks as he writes to Héloïse. This is also why a second time he suddenly begins to apostrophize his rebellious monks: "O my brethren, you who have embraced the monastic life . . . would that you would follow the example of these holy women whose weakness puts to shame your strength!" Why, it has been asked, does he address his monks as though he were among them?[30]—Reply: because that is where he is.

Thus one after the other these arguments collapse, like a house of cards, as soon as they are examined in the light of the original text of the Correspondence. Miss Charrier is quite sure what she would have answered in Héloïse's place. In a letter, authentic by her tastes, Héloïse ought to have reproached Abélard with all the infidelities referred to in the letter of Foulques and with the forced abandonment of the child in Brittany.[31] But, as we have already remarked, Foulques's charges are based on gossip. Perhaps Héloïse's reason for not reproaching Abélard with infidelity is that he simply was not guilty. As for abandoning the child in Brittany, she was hardly in a position to reproach him since she herself was equally guilty. Between Abélard and the child, she had chosen Abélard. Let us not use it against her, rather let us praise her prudence in not resorting to so dangerous an argument. Besides, the real issue lies elsewhere. Our task is not at all to rewrite Héloïse's letters as Miss Charrier would have written them, but to understand them as Héloïse wrote them. The internal contradictions that have been pointed out are all based on one single argument—the *nostrae conversionis* of Migne's *Patrology,* vol. 178, 184B. As Schmeidler puts it, this one point settles all the others, for "this correspondence is a whole, a work that is one even in its falseness: *ein einheitliches und einheitlich falsches Werk.*"[32] And Miss Charrier writes: "This correspondence forms a coherent whole. The improbability of the first letter, upon which all the others depend, entails the improbability of the entire correspondence."[33] If, however, there is no improbability in this letter, save in the minds of its critics, we must reverse the judgment against the Correspondence of Héloïse and Abélard. Since it is not, from beginning to end, apocryphal, then it is authentic from beginning to end: such are the exigencies of its perfect unity.

However, we are not yet at the end of our difficulties. When Schmeidler has shown to his own satisfaction that the correspondence of Héloïse is apocryphal, he naturally wondered who was its author. His answer is that Abélard wrote it. Why? Because the most striking characteristics of Abélard's style turn up in the so-called letters of Héloïse. Hence Abélard, if he did not write them, at least rewrote

taken place. Indeed, other reasons equally cogent point in quite the opposite direction.

Perseverance ultimately wins. Héloïse died twenty years after Abélard. Is it not possible to prove, if not that she is the author of the letters attributed to Abélard, at least that she revised them for circulation? In the first place, there is no doubt that she carefully collected souvenirs of Abélard.[39] Secondly, while the Abbot of Saint-Gildas, persecuted by his monks and then by the theologians who had him condemned, was living wretchedly in a Cluniac monastery, Héloïse could easily have put into shape this collection of letters in which her superiority is so evident. Finally, if Abélard had himself prepared the collection for his own purposes, how was it that he left unexpurgated those harsh, if true, passages in which Héloïse bared his egotism, his cruelty, his blindly stupid pride so often evidenced in this affair? It has been said that he wanted to show off his skill as a director of conscience. But the blunt fact is that in this he failed pitifully. Not once in all her letters did Héloïse ever admit that she accepted God's judgment as just, that she loved God more than Abélard, that it was for God and not for Abélard that she was doing expiation in the religious life. She did ultimately grow silent in the matter, but she never actually gave in. In her own eyes, her only greatness lay in this fact. This is what she would have others know, and in order to convince them she composed the collection of letters which we read today. Working as she did, with Abélard's writings ever in front of her, it is not surprising that she imitated his style, borrowed his quotations, his expressions, even his ideas. Héloïse was capable of doing this;

she had a motive for doing it; she (and she only) had the necessary time and leisure for it. Accordingly, she it was who wrote the whole correspondence.

This argument is no whit weaker than the other; but, let me hasten to add, it proves absolutely nothing. The correspondence of Héloïse and Abélard lies open in front of us. We can gloss it to our hearts' content, and search for newer and stranger hypotheses to explain its origin. A lot of this kind of thing has been done already, and no doubt the future will see a great deal more of it. But the wisest and most convincing of all hypotheses is that Héloïse is still the author of the letters of Héloïse and Abélard of those of Abélard. If there are decisive or even urgent reasons for admitting the contrary, they have not yet come to light, or if they have, I don't know where to find them. Assuredly it is neither to Lalanne's article nor Schmeidler's memoir, nor Miss Charrier's book that we are to turn in search of them.

Notes

Notes

Notes to the Introduction

[1] R. Rawlinson, *P. Abaelardi . . . et Heloissae . . . Epistolae,* a prioris editionis erroribus purgatae et cum cod. ms. collatae, Londini, E. Curll and W. Taylor, 1718. Reprinted at Oxford in 1728. Cf. Paris, Bibliothèque Nationale, Imprimés, Z, 13.801 and Z 13.802.

[2] Troyes, 802, f. 103 v: "Hunc librum emit Robertus de Bardis, cancellarius Parisiensis, anno 1346, in die beati Benedicti abbatis, cum 4 aliis libris de capitulo parisiensi."

[3] Denifle-Chatelain, *Chart. Univ. Paris.,* II, p. 460, n. 1.

[4] *Op cit.,* art. 1038; II, 501–2. Cf. art. 1039, p. 503.

[5] P. de Nolhac, *Pétrarque et l'Humanisme* (2ᵉ éd.; Paris, H. Champion, 1907), II, 219–20, n. 2.

[6] After a space of ten years we can acknowledge that the fruits have not this time exceeded the promise of the blossoms.

[7] However, one may consult with profit that splendid work on Abélard's teachings by J. G. Sikes, *Peter Abailard* (Cambridge, University Press, 1932).

[8] Charlotte Charrier, *Héloïse dans l'Histoire et dans la Légende* (Paris, H. Champion, 1933).

[9] The most accessible French translation, and the most pleasant to read, is that by Octave Gréard, *Lettres complètes d'Abélard et d'Héloïse* (Paris, Garnier, n.d.). The Latin-French edition of this work in the same library is at the moment out of print. The English translation, by Charles K. Scott Moncrieff, *The Letters of Abelard and Heloise* (London, Guy Chapman, 1925) is not very reliable.

Notes to Chapter One

¹ Abélard, *Hist. calam.*, cap. v, *PL* 178:126 A. For the colorful testimony of Foulques, see *Epist. ad Abaelardum*, PL 178: 371 C–372 C.

² Abélard, *Hist. calam.*, *PL* 178:126.

³ Foulques of Deuil, *op. cit.*, *PL* 178:372 C.

⁴ Abélard, *Dialogus*, *PL* 178:1613 C.

⁵ Charles de Rémusat, *Abélard*, I, 46, n. 2.

⁶ Charlotte Charrier, *Héloïse*, p. 128.

⁷ Foulques of Deuil, *Epist. ad Abaelardum*, *PL* 178:373 A.

⁸ Abélard, *Hist. calam.*, cap. v, *PL* 178:126 B.

⁹ *Op. cit.*, 126 C.

¹⁰ *Op. cit.*, cap. vi: 128 B.

¹¹ Roscelin, *Epistola*, *PL* 370 C. Cf. "ad meretricem transvolans" 370 D.

¹² Peter the Venerable, in V. Cousin, *P. Abaelardi . . . opera*, I, 710–11. Cf. Miss Charrier, pp. 58–59.

¹³ Abélard, *Hist. calam.*, cap. vi, *PL* 178:128 AB; Gréard's transl. pp. 11–12.

¹⁴ Ovid, *De arte amatoria*, II, 561 ff. Cf. V, 580.

¹⁵ Abélard, *Hist. calam.*, cap. vi, *PL* 178:129 B.

¹⁶ *Op. cit.*, col. 129 C.

¹⁷ Abélard, *Hist. calam.*, *PL* 178:130 A.

¹⁸ *Ibid.*, col. 132 B.

¹⁹ Abélard, Sermo III, *In circumcisione Domini*, *PL* 178: 406–7.

²⁰ The question will be clearly settled by St. Thomas: "Clericatus autem non est ordo, sed quaedam professio vitae dantium se divino ministerio". *De articulis fidei* in *Opuscula*, ed. Mandonnet III, 17. On the tonsure of clerics, see R. Génestal, *Le Privilegium Fori*, (Paris, Leroux, 1921), I, 3–4.

²¹ Isidore, *De ecclesiasticis officiis*, cap. iv, *PL* 83:442–43. Cf. Ivo of Chartres, *Decretum*, pars vi, cap. iv, *PL* 161:442–43. Cf.

Peter Lombard, *IV Sent.*, d. 24, cap. iv; ed. Quaracchi, p. 893: "clerici . . . id est sortiti."

[22] "Ideo ergo dicti sunt clerici, quia de sorte sunt Domini, vel quia Deum partem habent." Isidore, *Etymol.*, lib. vii, cap. xii, n. 1; *PL* 82:290. On St. Jerome, see p. 42, note 2.

[23] "La liaison (between *clericus* and *scholaris*) était si claire en droit que le mariage, en dissolvant l'état de cléricature, privait du droit d'enseigner." G. Paré, A. Brunet, P. Tremblay, *La Renaissance du XIIᵉ siècle* (Paris, 1933), p. 62.

[24] Ivo of Chartres, *Decretum*, VI, 51, *PL* 161:456.

[25] *Op. cit.*, VIII, 286; *PL* 161:646: "iterum tonderi cogatur, nec in vita sua tonsuram negligere audeat. . . . Si tonsuram dimiserit, rursum tondeatur."

[26] *Op. cit.*, VII, 115; *PL* 161:570.

[27] *Op. cit.*, VI, 51; *PL* 161:456. Cf. Gratian, *Decretum*, pars I, d. 32, cap. xiv; ed. Friedberg (Leipsig, 1879), col. 121.

[28] Abélard, *Epitome theologiae christianae*, cap. xxxi; *PL* 178:1746 CD. On the entire problem see A. Esmein, *Le mariage en droit canonique* (2ᵉ éd.; Paris, Recueil Sirey, 1929), I, 313–41. J. Dauvillier, *Le mariage dans le droit classique de l'Église* (Paris, Recueil Sirey, 1933), pp. 162–63.

[29] "Conjugium mali remedium est. Datur enim propter incontinentiam refrenandam; unde magis ad indulgentiam pertinet." Marriage is made by a "foederatio conjugii" in which one party says to the other: "Trado me tibi ad usum carnis meae, ita ut, quandiu vixeris, non me alii conjungam". *Op. cit.*, cap. xxxi; col. 1745.—"Conjugium etiam servitus dicitur. . . . Si autem liber, id est sine conjugio, ne accipias uxorem, si vis esse liber". *Ibid.*, col. 1746–47. The formula "nulli sapienti" appears in col. 1746 D. Cf. chapter II, note 4.

[30] *See* note 23 above.

[31] E. Vacandard, "Célibat" in *Dict. de théologie catholique*, col. 2085.

[32] Ivo of Chartres, *Decretum*, VI, 68; *PL* 161:459. Gratian, *Decretum*, pars I, d. 32, cap. viii; ed. Friedberg, col. 120.

[33] R. Génestal, *Le Privilegium Fori en France du Décret de*

Gratien à la fin du XIVe siècle, I, 82.—Cf. p. 84: in the twelfth century the married cleric can keep his functions if he wears the habit and tonsure.

[34] Canonical legislation has undergone a marked evolution in what concerns the right of married clerics to retain their benefices. It appears that the question was only definitively resolved in the negative after Alexander III [J. Freisen, *Geschichte des canonischen Eherechts* (2te Aufl., Paderborn, 1893), p. 746.] Beginning with Gregory IX, all hesitancy disappeared (*ibid.*, p. 747) and this is the way in which Abélard himself settled the question. But we must distinguish between the *beneficium* and the *officium*. A deacon who refused to observe continency lost at the same time his benefice and his function (Gratian, *Decretum*, pars I, d. 32, cap. x, ed. Friedberg, col. 120). On the other hand, clerics, porters, lectors, exorcists, and acolytes whose situation was regular kept their rank and were not deprived of their functions (*ibid.*, cap. xiv; col. 121). In fact, the reply of Pope Gregory to St. Augustine of Canterbury expressly states that a cleric who had not received orders, if he was incapable of preserving continency, was obliged to marry and seek to earn his own living. "Si qui vero sunt clerici extra sacros ordines constituti, qui se non possunt continere, sortiri uxores debent, et stipendia sua exterius accipere. . . ." Gratian, *ibid.*, cap. iii, col. 117. Such, precisely, would have been Abélard's case.

[35] Abélard, *Hist. calam.*, cap. vii; *PL* 178:131 A.

[36] "Quot in ecclesiis vidimus canonicos episcopis suis reluctantes, cum ab eis ad sacros ordines cogerentur, et se indignos tantis ministeriis profitentes, nec omnino velle acquiescere?" etc. Abélard, *Epist. VIII, PL* 178:273 A.

[37] Charles de Rémusat, *Vie d'Abélard*, I, 39.

[38] Héloïse, *Epist. IV*, PL 178, col. 195 A: "te quidem Parisiis scholis praesidente".

[39] Some idea of how indefinite is the meaning of *scholasticus* is to be had by consulting F. Hurter, *Tableau des institutions et des mœurs de l'Église au moyen âge* (Paris, 1843), I, 433–35.

According to Hurter, the *scholasticus* "was entrusted rather with the inspection of schools than with the task of teaching in them himself, though he often undertook the latter of his own accord" (p. 434). Here it is a question of quite a different function from that of Abélard in the schools of Paris. On the subject of the organization of chapters, see P. Hinschius, *System des katolischen Kirchenrechts* (Berlin, Guttentag, 1878), I, 59–80. There is nothing to be found, in this remarkable work, which applies exactly to what we know from elsewhere was Abélard's case. The *Cartulaire de l'église Notre-Dame de Paris*, published by M. Guérard (Paris, 1850), rarely mentions the *scholasticus* and gives no information on the subject.

⁴⁰ On this point see J. Freisen, *Geschichte des canonischen Eherechts bis zum Verfall der Glossenlitteratur* (2ᵗᵉ Aufl.; Paderborn, 1893), p. 735 and 739–40. Cf. T. P. McLaughlin, C.S.B., *Le très ancien droit monastique de l'Occident* (Paris, Picard, 1935), pp. 112 and 147.

⁴¹ C. J. Hefele, *Histoire des conciles* (Paris, Letouzey, 1911), IV, 11–14 (L. XXI, art. 417) Cf. art. 418, pp. 20–25, on the ancient rule of Chrodegang.

⁴² C. J. Hefele, *op. cit.*, IV, 1167–68 (L. XXX, art. 555). Cf. p. 1177.

⁴³ In the course of the twelfth century, the chapters themselves gave up the common life and the individual members took up residence in private homes near the church. Cf. Hurter, *op. cit.*, p. 417.

⁴⁴ Foulques of Deuil, *Epistola, PL* 178:374 C: "plangit liberalium canonicorum multitudo".

⁴⁵ T. P. McLaughlin, "The Prohibition of Marriage Against Canons in the Early Twelfth Century", *Mediaeval Studies*, III (1941), 95, art. 3.

Notes to Chapter Two

¹ Charles de Rémusat, *Abélard, sa vie, sa philosophie et sa théologie*, I, 63–64.

² *Ibid.*, p. 60, n. 1, and p. 62.

³ Abélard, *Epist. VIII, PL* 178:310 C.

⁴ However, we must not conceal the tone in which Abélard speaks about these things: "This is why, say Jerome and Theophrastus, a wise man should not marry. You can try out other things before taking them; you can know, for example, what kind of horse you are getting before buying it. But you cannot try out a wife before marrying her". Abélard, *Epist. Theol. christianae*, cap. xxxi; *PL* 178:1746 D. Abélard borrows this graceful remark from Jerome, who borrowed it from Seneca, who, in his turn, borrowed it from the *De nuptiis* of Theophrastus.

⁵ St. Jerome, *De viris illustribus*, cap. xii; *PL* 23:662.

⁶ Indeed, St. Jerome's testimony is probably the oldest we can cite in defense of the authenticity of this apocryphal work. See C. Aubertin, *Sénèque et saint Paul. Étude sur les rapports supposés entre le philosophe et l'apôtre* (3ᵉ ed.; Paris, Didier, 1872), p. 358. The correspondence is printed on pp. 429–36. The text referred to by Jerome appears in Letter XI, p. 434.

⁷ Seneca, *De beneficiis*, I, ii. Actually, Seneca expressly holds that the philosopher has the right to preach more virtue than he practices. *De vita beata*, xvii–xviii.

⁸ Jerome, *Adversus Jovinianum*, I, 47; *PL* 23:288–91. See the fragments of Seneca's *De matrimonio* collected and cited by Jerome, in *L. A. Senecae Opera*, ed. F. Haase (Leipzig, Teubner, 1853), III, Fragm. xiii, pp. 428–34.

⁹ *Ibid.*, 48:291.

¹⁰ *Hist. calam.*, cap. vii, *PL* 178:130–31.

¹¹ St. Jerome, *op. cit.*, 48:291. Héloïse, *Hist. calam., loc cit.*, col. 131 A. Cf. Seneca, *De matrimonio*, ed. P. Haase, III, 430, n. 61.

¹² St. Jerome, *op. cit.*, 48: col. 291. Héloïse, *op. cit.*, col. 131 C.

¹³ St. Jerome, *De perpetua virginitate B. Mariae*, n. 20, *PL* 23: 214 AC.–Cf. *Epist.* 54, *ad Furiam*, n. 4–5, *PL* 22:551–52. Héloïse, *op. cit.*, col. 131 AB.

[14] "Unde et Seneca maximus ille paupertatis et continentiae sectator, et summus inter universos philosophos morum aedificator". Abélard, *Epist. VIII, PL* 178:297 B.

[15] Abélard, *Epist. XII,* 178:350 B: "Seneca maximus ille morum philosophus".

[16] Abélard, *Sermo 24, In conversione sancti Pauli, PL* 178: 535–36: "insignis ille tam eloquentia quam moribus Seneca".

[17] Abélard, *Sermo 33, De sancto Joanne Baptista, PL* 178: 592-93: "Seneca quippe maximus morum aedificatur". It is to be noted that Abélard here upholds the hierarchy between the philosopher and the Apostle, col. 592 B.

[18] Abélard, *Expositio in Epist. Pauli ad Romanos,* lib. I, cap. i, *PL* 178:790 BC.

[19] Abélard, *Introductio ad theologiam,* lib. I, cap. xxiv, *PL* 178:1033 "Seneca quoque inter universos philosophos, tam moralis doctrinae quam vitae gratiam adeptus". (Cf. *Lettres apocryphes,* Epist. VII, in Charles Aubertin, *Sénèque et saint Paul,* p. 432). Abélard cites this text again in *Theologia christiana,* lib. I, *PL* 178:1164 C.

[20] Seneca, *ad Lucilium,* Epist. LXXII. To examples drawn from St. Jerome, Héloïse adds that of Pythagoras, taken from St. Augustine's *De civitate Dei,* VIII, 2, *PL* 41:225.

[21] Seneca, *ad Lucilium,* Epist. LXXIV.

[22] In fact, as A. Esmein has clearly seen and proved, St. Paul's teaching completely governs the evolution of canon law concerning the marriage of clerics. "Christian opinion used to associate some kind of fatal impurity with sexual relations, even between husband and wife. Hence, married people were commanded to abstain from sexual relations whenever they wished to devote themselves to prayer. Now the priest ought to give himself up to prayer incessantly". A. Esmein, *Le mariage en droit canonique,* (2e ed.), I, 314. Cf. the text of St. Jerome, *Adversus Jovinianum,* cited by Gratian, *Decretum,* Pars I, dist. 31, cap. i, ed. Friedberg, col. III, reproduced by Ivo of Chartres, *Panormia,* lib. III, cap. xcvi, *PL* 161:1152.

[23] St. Jerome, *Adversus Jovinianum,* lib. I, n. 7, *PL* 23:230.

²⁴ St. Jerome, *Epist. XXII, ad Eustochium*, n. 22, *PL* 22:409.

²⁵ Héloïse, *in* Abélard, *Hist. calam., PL* 178:130 B.

²⁶ Abélard, *loc. cit.*, col. 130 B: "et se et me pariter humiliaret".

²⁷ It is not out of the way to mention here that in the grounds invoked by canonical texts to justify either the forbidding of marriage to major clerics or the falls resulting from the marriage of minor clerics, the basic argument usually has to do with the abandoning of the state of perfection which such marriages necessarily imply. Licit or not, marriage is a form of incontinence. By reason of this principle, not only is the marriage of major clerics forbidden, but also the ordaining of men who have married a second time (*See* Chap. I above). Similarly, it is decreed that major clerics who marry are to be deprived of their benefices. Cf. Ivo of Chartres, in A. Esmein, *op. cit.*, p. 329, n. 2: "clericus vero qui *postposita clericali continentia, de superiori ordine ad inferiorem descendit,* stipendia militiae clericalis amittat". Esmein, adds: "There is no doubt that this canon was at least a subdeacon". Possibly he was, but there is nothing to prove it. Cf. Ivo of Chartres, *Panormia*, lib. III, cap. ci, *PL* 161:1152 D.

²⁸ Abélard, *op. cit.*, cap. v, col. 126 B.

²⁹ *Ibid.*

³⁰ *Ibid.*, cap. vii, col. 132 B.

³¹ *Corpus juris*, Decret., Pars II, causa 12, q. 1; in the *Dict. de Théologie catholique*, art. "Clercs", col. 226.

³² Héloïse, *in* Abélard, *Hist. calam.*, cap. vii, *PL* 178:130 B.

³³ St. Jerome, *Epist. LII, ad Nepotianum*, n. 5, *PL* 22:531–32. Clerics are so called "quia de sorte sunt Domini, vel quia ipse Dominus sors, id est pars clericorum est" (531). Hence, absolute poverty, avoiding of women, etc. *(ibid.).* And farther on: "Praedicator continentiae, nuptias ne conciliet" (col. 539). —Cf. Ivo of Chartres, *Decretum*, Pars VI, cap. i, *PL* 161:439, and cap. iii, col. 439–42 (following Jerome *loc. cit.*, and Isidore, *De off. eccles.*, lib. II, cap. i).

[34] Abélard, *Sermo XXXIII, De sancto Joanne Baptista, PL* 178:5872.

[35] Héloïse has actually used three different arguments, all closely related: This marriage was *probrosum, onerosum,* et *inhonestum.* She means by this that Abélard, married, would not have at his disposal the resources necessary to live the sort of social life in keeping with his state.—Cf. *Hist. calam.,* cap. vii, *PL* 178:131 A: "ipsum consule honestae conversationis statum". Their life together would have lacked dignity.

[36] Abélard, *Problemata Heloissae,* Probl. 14, *PL* 178:701 D. St. Paul and St. Jerome are cited in support.

[37] Abélard, *op. cit.,* Probl. 42, *PL* 178:727 D.

[38] Héloïse, *Epist. II, PL* 178:185 A.

[39] Abélard, *Epist. V, PL* 178:208 A.

Notes to Chapter Three

[1] Abélard, *Hist. calamit.,* cap. vii, *PL* 178:134 A.

[2] *Ibid.,* col. 134 B and 135 B. Cf. *Epist. V,* col. 206 D.

[3] Abélard was wide awake when subjected to this mutilation. Cf. farther on, the passage relative to Origen, cap. xiv, col. 177 A. The extent and depth of the impression produced by this outrage is attested by the letter of Foulques of Deuil, *PL* 178:374 D. This letter is older than the *Historia calamitatum* and verifies its exactness on certain points.

[4] Two of Abélard's assailants, including his servant who had betrayed him, were arrested and condemned, by the ecclesiastical tribunal, to have their eyes taken out and to undergo the same mutilation as Abélard. See *Hist. Calam.,* cap. vii, *PL* 178: 135 A. Foulques's letter confirms this and tells us moreover that Fulbert, who denied all part in the outrage, was ordered to have his goods confiscated. Abélard seems to have thought this punishment inadequate and wanted to appeal the decision in the hope of obtaining a severer judgment. Foulques wrote him

in order to bring him to his senses. The bishop and the canons, he said, have done justice to the limit of their powers.

⁵ In the margin opposite this passage in the manuscript of the *Historia calamitatum* once in Petrarch's possession, there appears in large letters the word *solitudo*. See Bibl. Nationale, Fonds latin, 2923 f°. 9 v°.–Cf. *Hist. calam.*, cap. xi, *PL* 178:161 A. Petrarch counted Abélard among the friends of solitude, in his *De vita solitaria*, II, 7, 1, éd. Bâle, 1581, I, 278.

⁶ Abélard, *Sermo XXX, De Eleemosyna pro sanctimonialibus de Paraclito, PL* 178:564-69. See particularly col. 568 C-569 B: "Hoc vero monasterium noviter constructum, nec a divite quodam fundatum est, nec possessionibus ditatum. Quod tamen in divinis officiis, et disciplina regulari, non minori studio perseverare quam caetera Dei gratia novimus. Sed novella ejus atque adhuc tenera plantatio, vestris, ut crescat, colenda est eleemosynis". The speaker refers to his audience as *fratres* (564 A); hence no conclusions about its composition are possible.

⁷ We can get some idea of what these calumnies were like from Roscelin's disgraceful letter in which he accuses Abélard of making amends to his former mistress with the money he was making at the Paraclete: "plus utique remunerando stuprum praeteritum peccans, quam emendo futurum, et qua prius cum voluptate abutebaris, adhuc ex voluntate abuteris, sed Dei gratia ex necessitate non praevales. . . . Teste Deo et electis angelis loquor, quia commonachos tuos perhibentes audivi, quia, cum sero ad monasterium reddis, undecumque congregatam pecuniam de pretio falsitatis quam doces, calcato pudore ad meretricem transvolans deportas, stuprumque praeteritum impudenter remuneras" (*PL* 178:370 D).–"Ad hujus imperfecti hominis ignominiae cumulum vero pertinet, quod in sigillo, quo fetidas illas litteras sigillasti, imaginem dua capita habentem, unum viri, alterum mulieris, ipse formasti. Unde quis dubitet, quanto adhuc in eam ardeat amore qui tali eam capitum conjunctione non erubuit honorare" (372 A). This letter seems certainly to refer to the period when Abélard was teaching at

the Paraclete, before leaving for Saint-Gildas (cf. col. 370 C). But it sets the tone for the calumnies which may have beset Abélard when he was staying near Héloïse after his return to the Paraclete.

8 Abélard, *Hist. calam.*, cap. xv, *PL* 178:179 A.

Notes to Chapter Four

1 Abélard, *Epist. V*, *PL* 178:206 CD.

2 Héloïse, *in* Abélard, *Hist. calam.*, cap. vii, *PL* 178:131 B: "omnes sibi voluptates interdixerunt, ut in unius philosophiae requiescerent amplexibus".

3 *Ibid.*, col. 132 B: "ne obscenitatibus istis te impudenter atque irrevocabiliter immergas".

4 O. Gréard has thus translated *ipsa*, and, it seems, quite justifiably; *trad. cit.*, p. 18.

5 Héloïse, *in* Abélard, *Hist. calam.*, cap. vii, *PL* 178:132 D.

6 *Ibid.*

7 Héloïse, *Epist. II*, *PL* 178:185 A.

8 Abélard, *Hist. calam.*, cap. vii, *PL* 178:132 D: "cum meam deflectere non posset stultitiam nec me sustineret offendere".

9 Héloïse actually says more—your courtesan *(meretrix)*. But the word has a technical force here, being taken over from St. Jerome, *Epist. CXXVIII*, *PL* 22:1096.—Cf. "Meretrix (est) quae multorum libidini patet". Gratian, *Decretum*, Pars I, dist. 34, cap. xvi, ed. Friedberg, col. 129.—On the other hand: "Concubina autem hic ea intelligitur, quae cessantibus legalibus instrumentis unita est, et conjugali affectu asciscitur; hanc conjugem facit affectus, concubinam vero lex nominat". Gratian, *Decretum*, Pars I, dist. 34, cap iii, *ed. cit.*, 126. Then Gratian quotes the Council of Toledo (I, c. xvii): "Is, qui non habet uxorem, et pro uxore concubinam habet, a communione non repellatur, tamen ut unius mulieris, aut uxoris aut concubinae (ut ei placuerit) sit conjunctione contentus" *(Loc. cit.*, cap. iv, col. 126). See, *ibid.*, the important note of cap. iv in which

there is reported the opinion of Justinian (nov. 18, cap. v) determining the case when concubinage can be considered as a quasi-marriage or as a non-solemn marriage. For this, three conditions were required: that the man and the woman be celibates; that they have mutual fidelity, *neque a procreatione filiorum abhorrerent;* that they have the firm purpose of remaining thus united until death: Gratian, *Decretum, ed. cit.,* col. 125 note. The indulgence of contemporaries, and even of ecclesiastical authorities, towards Héloïse becomes a little less surprising when account is taken of this distinction. In a word, it is not an exaggeration to say that concubinage may have been considered in the Middle Ages, even from a religious point of view, as less radically different from marriage than it is now considered in the same circles. Hence, when Héloïse wished to push her thesis to the extreme, she was willing to call herself even *meretrix.* See *Epist. II, PL* 178:185 A.

[10] Héloïse, *Epist. II, PL* 178:184–85.

[11] Cicero, *De amicitia,* ix, xiv, xxvii: "omnis ejus fructus in ipso amore est".

[12] Étienne Gilson, *La théologie mystique de saint Bernard* (Paris, J. Vrin, 1934), pp. 20–24.

[13] Abélard, *Expositio in Epist. Pauli ad Romanos,* lib. III, *PL* 178:891 A–893 C. On this text, see *La théologie mystique de saint Bernard,* Appendix II, Abélard, pp. 183–89.

[14] Abélard, *Monita ad Astralabium, PL* 178:1762 AD.

[15] Héloïse, *Epist. II, PL* 168:186 A.

[16] Abélard, *Scito te ipsum,* cap. iii, *PL* 178:640 B.

[17] *Ibid.,* col. 645 C.

[18] *Ibid.,* cap. x, col. 652.

[19] *Ibid.,* cap. xiii, col. 653.

[20] *Ibid.,* cap. iii, col. 644 A.

[21] *Ibid.,* col. 638 C.

[22] This teaching comes, in the spirit of Abélard, from a purely dialectical interpretation, and hence totally wanting in the necessary moderation, from a number of texts of St. Augustine. Here are the principal texts: "Non ergo quid quisque

them, and consequently destroyed their genuineness. Most noteworthy is Abélard's characteristic misuse of the expressions *tam . . . quam*, or *tanto . . . quanto*. The same expressions reappear with equal frequency in the letters attributed to Héloïse. Therefore she did not write these letters.[34] Here, it is a question of a verifiable fact and the argument has a solid basis. It remains to examine its significance.

The fact of the case is that Héloïse makes the same generous use of these expressions as Abélard. The simplest conclusion to be drawn is that she contracted this literary mannerism from Abélard. There is nothing surprising in this. Devoted as she was to him, what is more credible than that she should imitate his style? Miss Charrier foresaw this objection to Schmeidler's thesis and did her best to refute it. Where, she asks, could Héloïse have acquired the mannerisms of Abélard's style? Her lessons with him were on other things; they were not collaborators. "There are those who will say that she could have acquired this resemblance of style by studying Abélard's writings? But the letters of Héloïse have no such labored manner."[35] Certainly not! But in her use of similar methods, in her devotion to the same authors, even to the same favorite texts, in those basic ideas and doctrines which she borrowed from him, Héloïse reveals herself the complete disciple of Abélard. No one doubts that she had read his writings, even that she had meditated at length upon them. Even what she had not actually read, she must often have heard from his lips. The simplest hypothesis, no matter how confirmed an individualist she was, is that she spontaneously assumed certain of Abélard's mannerisms. There is no justification for saying either that Abélard wrote, or even rewrote, her letters.

The weakness of arguments of this kind become evident
when our two critics, anxious to push their advantage, undertake to exhibit other findings familiar to the hypotheti-
cal editor of this correspondence. Schmeidler had already
noted the frequency of the appearance of words like *saltem*
("at least") and *obsecro* ("I beseech"). Miss Charrier undertook to count them. She found that Héloïse employs
saltem ten times, while Abélard employed it four times.[36]
What does this prove? Certainly not that Abélard wrote
Héloïse's letters, nor even that his style has left its mark on
that of his wife. Why not, on the contrary, conclude that
Héloïse wrote the letters of Abélard? And as for the frequency of the term *obsecro*, there are thirteen cases for
Héloïse against nine for Abélard. Again, what does this
prove? That the tendency towards obsecration is a little
stronger in a woman in love than in the man who is trying
to calm her? We might have surmised all this without the
arithmetical preliminaries. There is no particular point in
using these same figures against themselves, but it is extremely entertaining to do so.

Proof from unity of style is far less decisive in a matter
of this kind than proof by unity of content and thought.
Even Schmeidler concedes this. In fact, he goes so far as to
say that although we can, in a pinch, discuss the argument
from style, that based on ideas is far more effective.[37] Actually, if we carefully study the parallel columns arranged by
Miss Charrier according to Schmeidler's materials, many
reservations seem to be necessary. In certain cases, the
parallel usages are merely banal expressions borrowed from
classical authors. Héloïse and Abélard both use the rather
hackneyed phrase *siccis oculis* "with dry eyes". But where

is the student of Latin compostion who has not? Both
write *res ipsa clamat* "the thing speaks for itself". Agreed!
But so does Roscelin in his frightful libel on Abélard
(369B). Are we to suppose that he too reworked Héloïse's
letters? Actually, most of these texts represent not Abélard's ideas borrowed by Héloïse, but quotations which
they both employ. Schmeidler and Miss Charrier place
side by side the most heterogeneous materials without realizing that it is quite impossible to compare them in the same
frame of reference. For example, they point out that Héloïse and Abélard have both used the expression *pseudo-
apostolorum* "of false apostles". This is quite true. But they
neglect to add that the word comes from II Corinthians,
20:13 and that Abélard only uses it in his *Commentary on
the Epistle to the Romans*. Both, it is true, speak of "pearls
before swine" *(margaritas ante porcos)*, but the expression
is hardly rare, and both of them had read Matthew 6:6. It
should certainly have been noted that this was the source of
the expression. Both write: *sunt viae hominum quae viden-
tur rectae*, etc. . . . , it would have been worth noting that
it is from Proverbs 5, 4. The *non coronabitur* . . . etc. is
from II Timothy 2, 5. *Fateor imbecillitatem meam* "I
acknowledge my weakness" . . . etc. is in both a quotation
from St. Jerome,[38] though we are not told about this. At
other times, as Héloïse and Abélard cite their sources, it
is impossible not to recognize that both are reproducing a
text of St. Gregory, St. Jerome, or Macrobius. Such con-
cordances are not without interest, but they merely prove
that Héloïse and Abélard have remembered the same texts
or, to put it differently, that Héloïse borrowed Abélard's
quotations as readily as his style. They certainly do not

prove either that Abélard was the author of Héloïse's letters
or that he revised them for circulation. If it were worth
dwelling upon, a concordance of the ideas shared by Héloïse and Abélard would be important and significant in a
very different way from the mere lifting out of the quotations which they both use. Without much trouble we could
find many more such quotations, and far more striking ones
than those cited by Schmeidler in his critical study, because
it is so patent a fact that Héloïse was profoundly influenced
by Abélard's teachings. To be much surprised at this, we
should have to forget that she was Héloïse. But even this
does not justify the conclusion that she was not the real
author of the letters that have come down to us under her
name.

When we get to the bottom of things, we find ourselves
in the presence of a phenomenon not at all rare in historical
research—a faulty proof leading towards innumerable false
positions. Schmeidler, misled by Ludovic Lalanne, was
convinced of the unauthentic character of the letters on the
strength of a defective text arising out of two mistransla-
tions. Once he was sure that Héloïse could not have written the letters, he had to look for someone who could have
written them, and this brought him to Abélard. Assured
that Abélard was their author, he must have wondered why
Abélard wrote them, and, to be sure, reasons were not
wanting. It could be maintained that Abélard had wished
to make the most of himself, to have Héloïse contribute to
his glory, to make the whole world see that he had con-
verted her. . . . These are not such bad reasons, but they
explain only too admirably a fact that does not seem to have

faciat, sed quo animo faciat, considerandum est". St. Augustine, *De sermone Domini in Monte*, lib. II, cap. xiii, n. 46, *PL* 34: 1289.–Cf. "Nam ut noveritis ex animo quemque pendendum ad retributionem vel praemii vel poenae . . ." *Enarr. in Ps.* 40, n. 9, *PL* 35:460. In addition, Héloïse has expressly referred to Augustine's *De bono conjugali* (cap. xxi, 25-26, *PL* 40:390-91) as the source from which she derives this doctrine. (Cf. Héloïse, *Epist. VI, PL* 178:222 B-D). "Bonum enim opus intentio facit, intentionem fides dirigit. Non valde attendas quid homo faciat, sed quid cum facit aspiciat, quo lacertos optimae gubernationis dirigat". *Enarr. in Ps.* 31, 4, *PL* 36:259.

23 Héloïse, *Epist. II, PL* 178:186 AB: "Non enim rei effectus, sed efficientis affectus in crimine est; nec quae fiunt, sed quo animo fiunt, aequitas pensat".

24 "Non meas voluptates sed tuas adimplere studui". *Ibid.*, col. 184 D. *See* note 10 and text above for complete passage.

25 *Ibid.*, col. 186 BC. Cf. col. 188 A.

26 Héloïse, *Epist. IV, PL* 178:196 A: "me ille ut supra positas feminas in culpam ex consensu non traxit".

Notes to Chapter Five

1 Abélard, *Hist. calam.*, cap. viii, *PL* 178:135 B.

2 *Ibid.*, col. 136 A.

3 Héloïse, *Epist. IV, PL* 178:193 A. Her exact expression is *"monialem monacho et sacerdoti. . . ."*

4 Abélard, *Hist. calam.*, cap. xv, *PL* 178:179 C.

5 *Ibid.*, cap. x, col. 159 A.

6 *Ibid.*, cap. viii, col. 136–37: "omnibus me supra modum onerosum atque odiosum effeci".

7 Abélard, *Epist. XII, PL* 178:343–52.

8 "Cum autem in divina Scriptura non minorem mihi gratiam quam in saeculari Dominus contulisse videretur", Abélard, *Hist. calam.*, cap. viii, *PL* 178:138–39.

9 *Ibid.*, col. 136 C.

¹⁰ Héloïse, *Epist. II*, *PL* 178 : 184 B.

¹¹ Abélard, *Epist. III*, *PL* 178 : 187 B: "Quod post nostram a saeculo ad Deum conversionem nondum tibi aliquid consolationis vel exhortationis scripserim".

¹² It is while appealing to the example of St. Jerome, and claiming Marcella and Asella as precedents, that Héloïse asks Abélard forty-two questions on Holy Scripture (*PL* 178:677–78). The whole of Abélard's *Epistola IX* to the religious of the Paraclete is full of St. Jerome, and the names of Eustochium, Marcella, and Paula constantly appear. Why do some think that Héloïse may have learned Greek and Hebrew as well as Latin? Because Paula and her daughter Eustochium knew these languages (col. 331 AB). Moreover, Abélard himself made the following comparison: "quae (*sc.* Heloissa) non solum Latinae, verum etiam tam Hebraicae quam Graecae non expers litteraturae, sola hoc tempore illam trium linguarum adepta peritiam videtur, quae ab omnibus in beato Hieronymo, tanquam singularis gratia, praedicatur, et ab ipso in supradictis venerabilibus feminis maxime commendatur". Abélard, *Epist. IX*, *PL* 178:333 BC.

¹³ Abélard, *Epistola ad Heloissam*, *PL* 178:379–80.

¹⁴ I do not think that Oddoul succeeded in justifying Abélard's act of forcing Héloïse to take the veil. He ought, either out of human prudence, or, what is more, out of respect for Héloïse, to have left the initiative to her. On the other hand, I think that Oddoul was absolutely right in praising Abélard's spiritual direction. Certainly he was responsible for the complete sacrifice he was asking of Héloïse, but since the past was irreparable, he was right in demanding such sacrifice. Cf. Oddoul, in the work of M. and Mme Guizot, *Abailard et Héloïse*, p. 28–29.

¹⁵ Abélard, *Epist. III*, *PL* 178:187 BC.

¹⁶ Abélard, *Epist. V*, *PL* 178:199 C. The charge that Abélard was trying to win over Héloïse by flattery remains to be proved.

¹⁷ Abélard, *Epistle V*, *PL* 178:210 AC.

¹⁸ *Ibid.*, col. 199 A and 204 D.

¹⁹ "O si fas sit dici crudelem mihi per omnia Deum!" Héloïse, *Epist. IV, PL* 178:194 B.

²⁰ *Ibid.*, col. 194 B–195 B.

²¹ ". . . corpus tuum pariter et animam conterens". Abélard, *Epist. V, PL* 178:205 A.

²² Héloïse, *Epist. IV, PL* 178:196–97.

²³ *Pharsalia*, VIII, 74–76: ". . . Habes aditum mansurae in saecula famae: laudis in hoc sexu non legum jura nec arma, unica materia est conjux miser".

²⁴ Lucan, *Pharsalia*, IX, 111–12: ". . . saevumque arte complexa dolorem perfruitur lacrimis et amat pro conjuge luctum".

²⁵ Abélard, *Epist. III, PL* 178:187 B. In the sense defined earlier in note 13 and text.

²⁶ *Ibid.*, col. 187 C–188 B.

²⁷ *Ibid.*, col. 189 C.

²⁸ *Ibid.*, col. 190 C.

²⁹ *Ibid.*, col. 191 C–192 A.

³⁰ *Ibid.*, col. 192 AC.

³¹ Héloïse, *Epist. IV, PL* 178:173–74, citing Lucan, *Phars.*, II, 14–15: "Sit subitum quodcumque paras; sit caeca futuri mens hominum fati; liceat sperare timenti".

³² On the objection to this interpretation, see É. Gilson, "Dix variations sur un thème d'Héloïse", *Arch. d'hist. doct. et. litt. du moyen âge* (1939), p. 397 note.

³³ Abélard *Epist. V, PL* 178:204 C. Virgil, *Eclog. III*, 65: "et fugit ad salices, et se cupit ante videri".

³⁴ "Cum qua [amaritudine animi] mihi non placere, neque mecum ad beatitudinem pervenire. Sustinebis illuc me sine te pergere, quem etiam ad Vulcania profiteris te sequi velle?" Abélard, *Epist. V, PL* 178:205 A.

³⁵ "Nosti . . . id impudentissime tunc actum esse in tam reverendo loco et summae Virgini consecrato". That is, in a corner of the nuns' refectory at Argenteuil, "cum quod alias diverteremus non haberemus". Héloïse, it will be remembered, had at the time been disguised as a novice. Cf. *op. cit.*, col. 205 C.

³⁶ *Ibid.*, col. 206 D-207 C.
³⁷ Abélard, *Epist. V*, PL 178:210 AC. Cf. Lucan, *Pharsalia*
VIII, 84–85.
³⁸ *Ibid.*, col. 212 AC.

Notes to Chapter Six

¹ Henry Adams, *Mont-Saint-Michel and Chartres* (Cambridge, Mass., 1933), 283–84. This divinatory work was originally copyrighted in 1904.
² Lucan, *Pharsalia*, VIII, v, 94–96.
³ Abélard, *Hist. calam.*, cap. viii, PL 178:136.
⁴ Héloïse, *Epist. II*, PL 178:186–87.
⁵ Héloïse, *Epist. IV*, PL 178:198 CD.
⁶ Héloïse, *Epist. II*, PL 178:184 D.
⁷ These phrases expressing doubts derive from the fact that in order to solve the problem it is necessary to go beyond history into the psychology of religious vocations. There is no *historical* reply to a problem of this nature, but the facts themselves propose one. Héloïse thought that to love God meant to love Him as she loved Abélard. She also seems to have thought that a religious vocation made the convent a place of spiritual pleasures. Those who would like to have an idea of the complexity of such questions will do well to read the priceless article of Father Bruno, "Témoignages de l'expérience mystique nocturne", in *Études Carmélitaines*, 22ᵉ année, II (1937), 237–301. The text of St. Teresa of Avila which we cite is the epigraph of this remarkable work.
⁸ Besides the writings of Abélard, who was far from despairing of Héloïse and who bound his own salvation to that of his beloved, we have some letters about her by Peter the Venerable. One of these especially is a masterpiece of delicacy and spiritual beauty. Peter seems to have been put on the path of Héloïse and Abélard to console them after their encounter with St. Bernard. Bernard was an incomparable master for

saints, but Peter an unrivaled guide for sinners. To know this grand person and to love him as he deserves to be loved, one simply must read his *Epist. XXVIII, PL* 189:347 ff. His admiration for Héloïse is everywhere evident. It has been said that he wanted to flatter her. But why so? I see no signs of it. The simple fact is that he thought highly of her. Peter the Venerable was not naïve. He would not have regretted, as he did, that the Abbess of the Paraclete was not at Cluny, if he had not regarded her as an admirable abbess. Coming from the man who was not anxious to grant hospitality to Abélard until he had made his peace with St. Bernard, against whom they both had reason to complain, such testimony gives cause for reflection. *See also* Chap. VII.

⁹ This is why, as has been seen, Abélard thought it necessary to state precisely that in his case the pain had not been so terrible. Cf. Chap. III, note 2, and text.

¹⁰ Héloïse, *Epist. IV, PL* 178:196 AB: "utinam hujus praecipue commissi dignam agere valeam poenitentiam, ut poenae illi tuae vulneris illati ex longa saltem poenitentiae contritione vicem quoquo modo recompensare queam; et quod tu ad horam in corpore pertulisti, ego in omni vita, ut justum est, in contritione mentis suscipiam, et hoc tibi saltem modo, si non Deo, satisfaciam".

¹¹ *Ibid.*, col. 194 D–195 A. It is to be noted that if Abélard's marriage had not been legitimate, all this argument of Héloïse's would have been absurd, and Abélard would surely have called her attention to it.

¹² *Ibid.*, col. 196 B.

¹³ *Ibid.*, col. 196 B.

¹⁴ *Ibid.*, col. 196: "quae cum ingemiscere debeam de commissis, suspiro potius de amissis".

¹⁵ Cf. ". . . quia nihil prosit carnem habere virginem, si mente nupserit". St. Jerome, *De perp. virginit. B. Mariae*, 20, *PL* 23:214 A.

¹⁶ *Ibid.*, col. 197 A–198 D: "diu te, sicut multos, simulatio mea fefellit, ut religioni deputares hypocrisin".

[17] Héloïse, *Epist. VI, PL* 178:213 A: "ne me forte in aliquo de inobedientia causari queas".

[18] Héloïse, *Epist. II, PL* 178:181 B.

[19] Héloïse, *Epist. IV, PL* 178:191 D.

[20] Héloïse, *Epist. VI, PL* 178:213 A. On the meaning of this expression, see Charles de Rémusat, *Abélard,* I, 160. De Rémusat has translated it well as: "A Dieu par l'espèce, à lui comme individu", that is, "the nun is God's, the wife yours".

[21] Charles de Rémusat, *Abélard,* I, 160.

[22] For a picture of the kind of life that was led in the Paraclete, see the simple and moving documents published in Migne, *PL* 178:313 C–317 A. These lines have been attributed to Héloïse, but as there is some uncertainty in the matter, I have not used them, helpful and suggestive as they are.

Notes to Chapter Seven

[1] Peter the Venerable, *Epist. I,* 27, *PL* 189:116.

[2] Peter the Venerable, *Epist. IV,* 4, *PL* 189:305–6.

[3] A. de Lamartine, *Héloïse et Abélard* (Paris, 1859), p. 49.

[4] Charles de Rémusat, *Abélard,* I, 258.

[5] Peter the Venerable, *Epist. IV,* 21, *PL* 189:346–53: "hunc, inquam, loco tui vel ut te alteram in gremio suo confovet".

[6] Cf. *PL* 189:487, p. 182.

[7] Peter the Venerable, *Epist. VI,* 22, *PL* 189:428–29. See the letter of Héloïse to the Abbot of Cluny, *Epist. 21,* col. 427–28.

Notes to Chapter Eight

[1] Jacob Burckhardt, *The Civilisation of the Renaissance in Italy* (London, Harrap, 1929), p. 303.

[2] *Ibid.,* p. 303.

[3] *Ibid.,* p. 308.

[4] P. de Nolhac, *Pétrarque et l'Humanisme* (2e ed.; Paris, Leroux, 1907), I, 2.

[5] Burckhardt, *op. cit.*, p. 328.

[6] G. Voigt, *Pétrarque, Boccace et les débuts de l'humanisme en Italie* (Paris, Welter, 1894), p. 10.

[7] It is perfectly clear that biography began well before the fourteenth century, as Burckhardt knows. But as we shall see later on, there are facts which count and facts which don't count. Thus we find Burckhardt saying (*op. cit.*, p. 324) of Joinville's *Life of St. Louis* that it is a book unique in kind and "the first complete spiritual portrait of a modern European nature". Having noted this fact which, incidentally, destroys his thesis, Burckhardt continues to write as though this fact had never existed.

[8] Burckhardt, *op. cit.*, p. 330.

[9] Gustave Cohen, *Ronsard, sa vie et son œuvre* (Paris, Boivin, 1924), 286–87.

[10] Cited by A. Lefranc, "Diverses définitions de la Renaissance", *Revue des Cours et Conférences*, 18e année, II (n°. 28, 1910), 490.

[11] A. Lefranc, *op. cit.*, p. 494.

[12] A. Lefranc in *Revue des Cours et Conférences*, 1909–1910, II, 725; quoted by G. Cohen, *Ronsard* . . . , p. 9, note 3. The phrase we quote next appears on p. 10.

[13] É. Gilson, *Les Idées et les Lettres*, 1re série, (Paris, J. Vrin, 1932), pp. 197–241. Very important is the decisive work of L. Febvre, *Le problème de l'incroyance au XVIe siècle*, (Paris, Albin Michel, 1942).

[14] M. Citoleux, *Le vrai Montaigne, théologien et soldat* (Paris, P. Lethielleux, 1937), p. 68.

[15] *Chartul. Universitatis Parisiensis*, I, 541, n. 470.

[16] G. Cohen, *Ronsard* . . . , p. 284.

[17] Etienne Gilson, "La cosmogonie de Bernardus Silvestris", *Arch. d'hist. doctr. et litt. du Moyen Âge*, III (1928), 21.

[18] Thomas Aquinas, *In Physic. Arist.*, I, ix, 15, art. 11: "Impossibile est materiam primam generari vel corrumpi".

[19] G. Cohen, *Ronsard* . . . , p. 285.

[20] J. Nordström, *Moyen Âge et Renaissance* (Paris, Stock, 1933), pp. 113–14.

[21] No doubt mindful of St. Jerome, *Epist. CXXV*, 14; *PL* 22: 1080.

[22] Héloïse, *Epist. VI; PL* 178 : 214 B. Cf. Ovid, *De arte amandi*, I, 233. [Gilson is citing the French translation of M. H. Bornecque, Ovide, *L'Art d'aimer* (Paris, Les Belles Lettres, 1924), p. 11.] For verse 244, we are following the reading: *in vinis* rather than the *in venis* of Migne. In the absence of a critical edition of Héloïse's letter, it is hard to tell which reading she had used.

[23] Héloïse, *op. cit.*, col. 214 B–215 A.

[24] Héloïse, *op. cit.*, col. 215 A.

[25] Héloïse, *op. cit.*, col. 216 B.

[26] In *Epistola VI*, Héloïse was proposing a monastic rule in conformity with Abélard's fundamental principles. It is again a case where the "théologie du couple" comes into play. Relying on the *Contra Jovinianum* of St. Jerome, Abélard had praised highly the virtues of the ancient philosophers. For philosophy is a life more than a science (*Theologia Christiana*, II; *PL* 178 : 1178 C); their life and teaching is little, or not at all, removed from Christianity (1179 B). Indeed, "si diligenter moralia Evangelii praecepta consideremus, *nihil ea aliud quam reformationem legis naturalis inveniemus*, quam secutos esse philosophos constat, cum lex magis figuralibus quam moralibus nitatur mandatis, et exteriori potius justitia, quam interiori abundet evangelium vero virtutes ac vitia diligenter examinat, et secundum animi intentionem omnia, sicut et philosophi, pensat" (1179 D). This interpretation of the law of the Gospels as a reformation or restoration of natural law, and the anti-Jewish hostility which derives from it, lie behind all Héloïse's propositions. But the Abbot of Saint-Gildas was no longer the man who had written the *Theologia Christiana*, nor, moreover, was the problem still the same problem. It was a question this time of settling upon a rule which might satisfy the requirements of the Gospels, rather than that single continence which now becomes the characteristic mark of monastic life. Abélard's principle would be interpreted in two senses. Either it

demands of layfolk all the observances imposed upon monks, or it concedes to monks all the liberties accorded layfolk. In either case, we should end up by eliminating monastic observance as such and by denying that there could be any difference whatsoever between a *monastic* life and a *Christian* life, except always for continence. Even on this point, we must note in Abélard, and above all in Héloïse, a tendency to raise Christian marriage to the plane of the *De bono conjugali* of St. Augustine.

²⁷ Héloïse, *op. cit.*, col. 216 D: "quisquis evangelicis praeceptis continentiae virtutem addiderit, monasticam perfectionem implebit".

²⁸ Héloïse, *op. cit.*, col. 216–17: "Atque utinam ad hoc nostra religio conscendere posset ut Evangelium impleret, non transcenderet, ne plusquam Christianae appeteremus esse".

²⁹ Cf. Erasmus, *Colloquia*, esp. *Franciscani* et *Ictyophagi*, with Héloïse, *Epist. VI, PL* 178:220 C–222 A.

³⁰ On the Stoic teaching on *indifferentia* see Seneca, *Ad Lucilium, Epist. CXVII*, and St. Jerome, *Ad Augustinum*, n. 16; *PL* 22:926.

³¹ Héloïse, *op. cit.*, col. 222 B: "nihil meritis superaddunt opera".

³² Héloïse, *op. cit.*, col. 222–23.

³³ Héloïse, *op. cit.*, col. 218 C.

³⁴ Héloïse, *op. cit.*, col. 224 A: "quae sunt exterius et indifferentia vocantur".

³⁵ Abélard, *Epist. VIII*, col. 283 C.

³⁶ Abélard, *Epist. VIII*, col. 293 C: "naturam sequens potius quam trahens". The study of Abélard's monastic ideal and its sources has still to be done. It will be an important work when it is done, and Seneca's *Epist. V, ad Lucilium* will play an essential role in it. Such a study will raise one very difficult problem. For Abélard, the monk can say with Seneca: "propositum nostrum est, secundum naturam vivere" *(op. cit.)*. But his idea of a quasi-Christian Seneca led him to impose upon laymen an austerity of life which many a monk would regard as quite

sufficient rather than to think of the monk's life much as laymen, even Christian laymen, think of theirs. Abélard's theoretic
laxism is not incompatible with the actual rigorism he set up for
himself and imposed upon Héloïse. Erasmus later used similar
theoretical principles, but applied them less rigorously. But
Abélard did not completely "monachize" laymen nor did Erasmus completely laicize monks. Neither of them completely
Christianized nor paganized Seneca. They were both seeking
one of the many possible states of equilibrium in the complexity
of Christian humanism. On Seneca's tendencies towards rigorism see *Epist. ad Lucilium*, CVIII.

[37] Lucan, *Pharsalia*, III, 23.

[38] *Op. cit.*, VIII, 639: O conjux, ego te scelerata peremi".

[39] Plutarch, *Life of Pompey*, Chap. LV. See M. A. Bourgery's
note in his edition of the *Pharsalia*, I, p. 165, n. 1.

Notes to the Appendix

[1] See the note of Ludovic Lalanne, *La Correspondance littéraire*, I (5 mars 1857), p. 109, n. 2.

[2] Lalanne acknowledges embarrassment, for if some passages
cannot have been written as they stand by Héloïse, at least in
the period which must be assigned them according to the letters, "there are others, and they are far more numerous, which
seem to be unattackable". He proves, therefore, that the correspondence was leisurely edited by Héloïse after Abélard's
death, but from the letters which she had, at various times,
either written or received: L. Lalanne, "Quelques doutes sur
l'authenticité de la correspondance amoureuse d'Héloïse et
d'Abélard", in *La Correspondance littéraire*, I (5 déc. 1856), p.
32–33. There may be some truth in this supposition.

[3] L. Lalanne, *art. cit.*, p. 30.

[4] B. Hauréau's reply to Lalanne deals with another point.
Refusing to discuss the problem of the authenticity of the letters, he restricts himself to pointing out a text which proves that

Abélard was Abbot of Saint-Gildas in 1127. See *La Corre-spondance littéraire*, I (5 Mars 1857), p. 110.

[5] B. Schmeidler, "Der Briefwechsel zwischen Abélard und Héloïse eine Fälschung?", *Archiv. für Kulturgeschichte*, XI (1913), 1–30. Cf. p. 7, note 1.

[6] Charlotte Charrier, *Héloïse dans l'histoire et dans la légende* (Paris, H. Champion, 1933). Cf. "Nous adoptons pleinement l'opinion de M. Schmeidler", p. 13.

[7] Schmeidler, *op. cit.*, pp. 3–5. Taken up again by Miss Charrier, *op. cit.*, pp. 13–15.

[8] V. Cousin, *P. Abaelardi opera*, I, 74 and 76.–Cf. Migne, *PL* 178:184 B and 186 B.

[9] Lalanne, *art. cit.*, p. 30.

[10] M. and Mme Guizot, *Abailard et Héloïse, essai historique . . . suivi des Lettres d'Abailard et d'Héloïse traduites sur les manuscrits de la Bibilothèque royale par M. Oddoul* (nouvelle édit. entièrement refondue; Paris, Didier, 1853), p. 111.

[11] O. Gréard, *Lettres complètes d'Abélard et d' Héloïse* (traduction nouvelle précédée d' une Préface; Paris, Garnier, s.d.), p. 59.

[12] Charrier, *op. cit.*, p. 14.

[13] It is possible to go back farther yet to Dom Gervaise, *Lettres véritables d'Héloïse et d'Abélard* (2 vol.; Paris, Musier, 1723).–Cf. I, 38–39.

[14] Abélard, *Epist. III; PL* 178:187 B. This phrase with which Abélard's letter opens is a reply to the close of Héloïse's letter, 186 B–188 A.

[15] It is here a question of letters of direction such as those written by St. Ambrose and St. Jerome to those under their direction. Strictly speaking, the phrase does not even exclude the possibility of an exchange of letters, now lost, which would only have contained news. For example, Abélard could have written to Héloïse to acquaint her with his plan to give her the Paraclete and summon her to it, without any contradiction with the phrases we have analyzed.

[16] D. C. Butler, *Le monachisme bénédictin* (Paris, de Gigord,

1924), pp. 144–45. Cf. B. Linderbauer, *S. Benedicti Regula monasteriorum* (Bonn, 1928), I, 8; lviii, 2 and 26; lxiii, 4 and 5.

[17] For example: "nostra autem conversatio in coelis . . ." *Philipp.*, III, 30.

[18] "post conversionem Berengarii patris mei ad professionem monasticam" (122 A).—"nostrae conversionis miserabilem historiam" (181 B).—"post nostram a saeculo ad Deum conversionem" (187 B).—"de nostrae conversionis modo" (204 D).— "in hoc videlicet nostrae conversionis modo" (205 B).

[19] Bibl. Nat., Fonds latin, 2544 f°. 14 v. *b;* and 2923, f°. 15 r. *a;* these are fourteenth-century manuscripts. The Reims ms., 872, also reads *conversationis* in all letters, and *conversionem* (f°. 124 r° and 128 v°). Only Troyes 802 gives *conversionis* and *conversionem* (f°. 19 v° and 20 v°) and it is this faulty reading which has unfortunately prevailed. The last two manuscripts are generally assigned to the thirteenth century without any decisive reason. They could belong to the fourteenth century like those of Paris.

[20] Abélard installed Héloïse in the Paraclete in 1129. Abélard had not returned to Brittany on January 20, 1131, since this is the date of his meeting with Pope Innocent II in the Abbey of Morigny near Étampes. We do not know when he returned to Saint-Gildas. The whole of the end of the *Historia calamitatum* attests his presence there when writing this letter: "In quo etiam adhuc laboro periculo" etc., (col. 180 B). Since his return to Saint-Gildas, he has had time: to be so persecuted by his monks that he had to resolve to leave his abbey and to incur excommunication; to obtain from his rebellious monks their promise to depart, thanks to the support of a pontifical legate come for that very purpose; to expel them afterwards because they refused to depart; to return to his abbey where he had to say that those who had remained were worse than those who had gone. Some time was necessary for these events to take place. How much? We do not know. Nor do we know on what exact date Abélard returned to Paris. We only know from John of Salisbury that he was teaching there again in 1136. Between 1131

and 1136, in whatever epoch we put him, a silence of one or two years was quite enough for Héloïse to find the time long. We need nothing more than this to justify the *jamdudum* which she uses.

²¹ On the other hand, the fifteenth-century manuscript, Nouv. Acquis. lat. 1873, f°. 157 r°, gives *conversationem*. This variant can be justified by giving it the meaning of *conversionem*, which is not impossible. If we wished to keep the usual sense of *conversationem*, we should have to conclude that even the text 186 B does not apply to the religious profession of Abélard and Héloïse but to Héloïse's installation in the Paraclete. This is hardly credible, given Abélard's reply (187 B). It is to be noted that for the following passage, 186 C, where *conversationis* is the natural term, the MSS. 1873, 2544, 2545 and 2923 are one in giving it.

²² Schmeidler, *op. cit.*, p. 5, note 3.

²³ Schmeidler, *op. cit.*, p. 6.

²⁴ Charrier, *op. cit.*, pp. 16–17.

²⁵ Charrier, *op. cit.*, pp. 17–18.

²⁶ Charrier, *op. cit.*, p. 18.—Borrowed from Schmeidler, *op. cit.*, p. 18.

²⁷ Abélard, *Epist. III, PL* 178:187 C.

²⁸ Charrier, *op. cit.*, p. 17.

²⁹ Abélard, *Hist. calam.*, cap. xv; *PL* 178:179 B.

³⁰ Charrier, *op. cit.*, p. 18.—Schmeidler, *op. cit.*, p. 27.

³¹ Charrier, *loc. cit.* Other reproaches are even more amusing, especially that on p. 19 which rests on the very modern hypothesis that it was impossible to quote Lucan or Ovid correctly without having the text on hand. Those who could do this even today are not so rare as Miss Charrier seems to think.

³² Schmeidler, *op. cit.*, p. 7.

³³ Charrier, *op. cit.*, p. 15.

³⁴ Schmeidler, *op. cit.*, pp. 8–10 and pp. 16–19.—Charrier, *op. cit.* pp. 19–20 and 573–76.

³⁵ Charrier, *op. cit.*, p. 22, note 7. Schmeidler refuses even to discuss the question. Indeed, *since* [for Schmeidler] *there can*

*be no question that Héloïse was the author of the letters attrib-
uted to him*, there is hardly any point in asking whether she
imitated Abélard in writing them: *op. cit.*, pp. 11-12. Simple
enough, as we see.

[36] Charrier, *op. cit.*, pp. 576–77.

[37] Schmeidler, *op. cit.*, p. 20.

[38] St. Jerome, *ad Heliodorum*, quoted by Abélard, *Epist.
XII, PL* 178:198 D.

[39] It seems certain that Héloïse no longer had the *Historia
calamitatum* before her when she was writing her first reply.
For she writes: "Erant, *memini*, hujus epistolae fere omnia felle
et absynthio plena" (*Epist. II, PL* 178:181 B). But it was a long
text to copy and we don't know how long she had the *Historia*
at her disposal. This fact in no way justifies Lalanne's hypothesis that there is literary artifice in this passage (Lalanne, *art. cit.*,
p. 30). On the other hand, Lalanne makes a more likely hypothesis than Schmeidler and Miss Charrier when he supposes
that it was Héloïse and not Abélard who worked over this correspondence (*art. cit.*, p. 32). If anyone did this, the chances
are it was she. Even if she only gathered the letters together
and made a collection of them, it is clear she could not have
done so without rereading them. In rereading them, she might
have corrected details as anyone does on rereading their letters. But we know nothing about this. Arguments hitherto
used to prove this are extremely vague or are based on confusion. The improbabilities and contradictions do not lie in the
text of Abélard and Héloïse but in that of their critics.